TALK TO THE DEAF

A Manual of Approximately 1,000 Signs
Used by the Deaf of North America

By

LOTTIE L. RIEKEHOF

Illustrated
by
BETTY STEWART

Art Advisor, Warren B. Straton

GOSPEL PUBLISHING HOUSE
1445 Boonville Ave., Springfield, Mo. 65802
02-0612

FOREWORD

Of all the means of communication used by the deaf, the least understood by the general public is the use of signs and finger spelling, especially the use of signs. The clarity and beauty of expression in proper use of the sign language cannot be surpassed. Its advantages extend beyond the realm of the deaf, for it has been found useful by people with speech loss due to neurological involvement, by laryngectomees and even by skin divers for underwater communication. In fact, the full extent of its usefulness has yet to be explored.

The need for human beings to communicate is one of the most basic needs. There are a great number of deaf children who are not able to meet the pace required for oral speech and, therefore, there is a need for implementation in their means of communication. Rigidly enforced restriction of communication in the early years of childhood of these children could conceivably have psychological implications. Enthusiasm for teaching speech to the deaf has increased through the years, and this is necessary in order to prepare the deaf child to take his place in society. However, the deaf child must be trained in all areas of living and must be given the opportunity to mature to his greatest capacity. Thus, in his all-around education the child's development outside of the classroom in the use of signs and finger spelling will often go hand in hand with his classroom development of oral communication.

There is some public opinion that those who use the manual means of communication have not done so well educationally. Dr. Helmer Myklebust, Professor of Audiology at Northwestern University, feels that those who use this means of communication turn out just as well in educational achievement as any other. The capabilities of the youngster are the deciding factor, not merely the means of communication.

Alexander Graham Bell, who appeared before a Royal Commission in 1888 to give evidence on teaching the deaf, commented, "For we want that method, whatever it is, that will give us the readiest and quickest means of bringing English words to the eyes of the deaf, and I know of no more expeditious means than a manual alphabet."

Since man is a social being, it is important that he develop a means of communicating with others, including the deaf. It is not difficult to learn the manual alphabet and the sign language and it will pay dividends to both the deaf and the hearing who are interested in the welfare of their fellow man.

Stanley D. Roth, Litt.D.
Superintendent of the Kansas School for the
Deaf; Member of Executive Board of the
Conference of Executives of American
Schools for the Deaf

ABOUT THE AUTHOR

The author of this unique book, Lottie L. Riekehof, is dean of women and associate professor at the world's only liberal arts college for the deaf, Gallaudet College in Washington, D.C. She originally studied at the college under the late Dr. Elizabeth Peet, long considered America's leading authority on the language of signs.

Before joining the Gallaudet College faculty Dr. Riekehof was engaged in teaching and research at the New York University Center for Research and Training in Deafness. Both her M.A. and Ph. D. degrees were earned at the University.

Dr. Riekehof's interest in the education of the deaf has continued since her first association with deaf people in the Washington area. After several years of activity with the deaf in New York, New Jersey, and Washington she accepted an invitation to join the faculty of Central Bible College in Springfield, Missouri, where she served as dean of women and was actively engaged in the training of deaf students, first through interpreters and later in a special diploma program which she helped to initiate.

Both hearing and deaf students who have studied the sign language with Dr. Riekehof are now active in work with the deaf in educational, religious, and social fields. Her book has been in demand ever since its first printing and is considered one of the best texts available for the beginning student in sign language.

CONTENTS

A BRIEF HISTORY OF THE SIGN LANGUAGE

The sign language used by the deaf in the United States was brought to America from France early in the 19th century. Dr. Thomas Hopkins Gallaudet, who was instrumental in bringing the sign language to this country, first became interested in the deaf through Alice Cogswell, a deaf child from New England. Dr. Gallaudet was sent to Europe by a group of interested American citizens and after a visit with British educators of the deaf, which proved unsuccessful, he crossed the Channel and visited a school for the deaf in Paris. This school had been founded in 1755 by Abbé de l'Epée who is said to have been the inventor of the sign language. The Abbé's system of sign language was based primarily on natural pantomime but many signs were purely arbitrary. Dr. Gallaudet spent some time at the French school with the Abbé Sicard, who was then in charge of the school, studying their methods of teaching the deaf and learning their sign language. He then returned to America, bringing back with him Laurent Clerc, a young deaf instructor from the French school. Upon their return, Dr. Gallaudet established the first permanent school for the deaf in Hartford, Connecticut, in 1817.

In the American schools today sign language is not taught. However, in many residential schools for the deaf the language of signs is permitted in public assemblies so that the children may have the opportunity of understanding guest speakers through interpreters. In these schools the sign language is also permitted in the dormitories, on the playground, and in social activities. However, in the classroom intensive effort is made to communicate orally so that development is made by the child in speech and in speech reading. Since it is possible for a person to speak, sign, and use the manual alphabet simultaneously, the "simultaneous method" of instruction is used in the advanced classes of many of the state residential schools as it also is at Gallaudet College in Washington, D. C., which is the world's only college for the deaf.

LEARNING TO USE THE SIGN LANGUAGE
AND THE MANUAL ALPHABET

The sign language, being a language of natural gesture and pantomime can be easily learned since there is so much obvious relationship between the sign and the meaning. The gestures are made with the use of the hands and arms, combined with appropriate facial expression. Graceful sign-making is an art which can be mastered and used effectively by both deaf and hearing persons. It is thus possible for hearing people to break the language barrier and communicate easily with the deaf. Most public speakers to the deaf use a combination of speech, signs, and the manual alphabet.

First, and all-important, is the mastery of the manual alphabet, the use of which is called finger-spelling. In order to form the letters of the alphabet properly, the palm of the hand should face the audience with the arm being held in an easy position near the body. It is not necessary to move the arm but some motion is permissible. Each letter should be made clearly and distinctly with a slight pause between words. Possessives are indicated by adding an "s" to the end of the word and twisting the wrist so that the fingers and thumb are facing up, still in the "s" position. When making double letters, as in "summer," "letter," "cool," etc., the hand is opened slightly before repeating the second letter of the series. Capitalized abbreviations, such as U.S.A., are indicated by circling each letter in a clockwise motion.

The signs described in this manual are a compilation of those most commonly used by the deaf of North America. Although local differences do exist, the descriptions herein presented have been chosen because they seem most accurate and are those used by expert sign-makers across the country. In many instances the root meaning or "idea" of the sign is given immediately following the description. This will help those learning sign language to quickly and easily associate the sign with the idea, making it easier to remember the sign. Since signs convey ideas rather than words, a number of synonyms are often given. A complete list of such synonyms has not been made, but enough are listed so that the true meaning of the sign is made clear. A sign does not exist for every word, but a good signer will be resourceful and choose the most appropriate sign and the one which most nearly expresses the desired thought. The expert is not necessarily the person who knows the greatest number of signs but rather the one who chooses his signs carefully.

The use of "initial" signs is a great help in being specific. Such signs are made by beginning the sign with the first letter of the desired word. For example, the sign for "think" is made by revolving the index finger before the forehead. This can also mean "meditate" or other related synonyms. However, when this motion is made using an "r" instead of the index finger, it stands for the specific noun "reason" and has no synonym. Signs acquire specific meaning only when they are "initial" signs or when they are associated with other signs or spelled words.

Plurals, tenses and word endings are not indicated except through context or by adding the word "finished" to indicate the past tense. To illustrate, the same sign is used for "teach," "taught," and teaching." However, there is a word ending to indicate the person when the word "teacher" is signed. This is described on page 98.

Movements should be free and graceful rather than stiff or angular. The size of the signs depends on the size of the group to which one is speaking. With a large audience, large signs must be made with good lighting on the speaker. With a conversational group of two or three people, signs are naturally reduced in size. Facial expression and emphasis in movement are very important. For example, a pleasant expression on the face combined with the sign for "pleasure" indicates that one is enjoying something. However, a frown or shaking of the head negatively while making the same sign shows that one has no pleasure or does not like something. The sign for "request" is identical with the sign for "demand" but it is necessary to use more emphasis for the latter to indicate that particular meaning.

In order to learn the signs accurately from this manual, it is important to study both the written instructions and the drawing. One is not complete without the other. It is almost impossible to indicate every movement of a sign on a single picture and therefore the written description is provided. Note that in all front-view drawings, the sign is made facing you and therefore the right hand in the picture will be to your left and vice versa.

Signs have been grouped into the categories in which they most naturally fall in order that they may be learned by association with other signs of similar meaning. Occasionally synonyms and antonyms have been listed together in order to facilitate learning. The complete alphabetical index in the last pages of the book will be an indispensable aid in locating a sign. If the desired word is not listed, the word nearest in meaning should be found.

MANUAL ALPHABET

 A

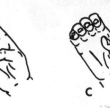 B

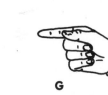 C

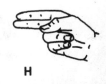 D

 E

 F

 G

 H

 I

 J

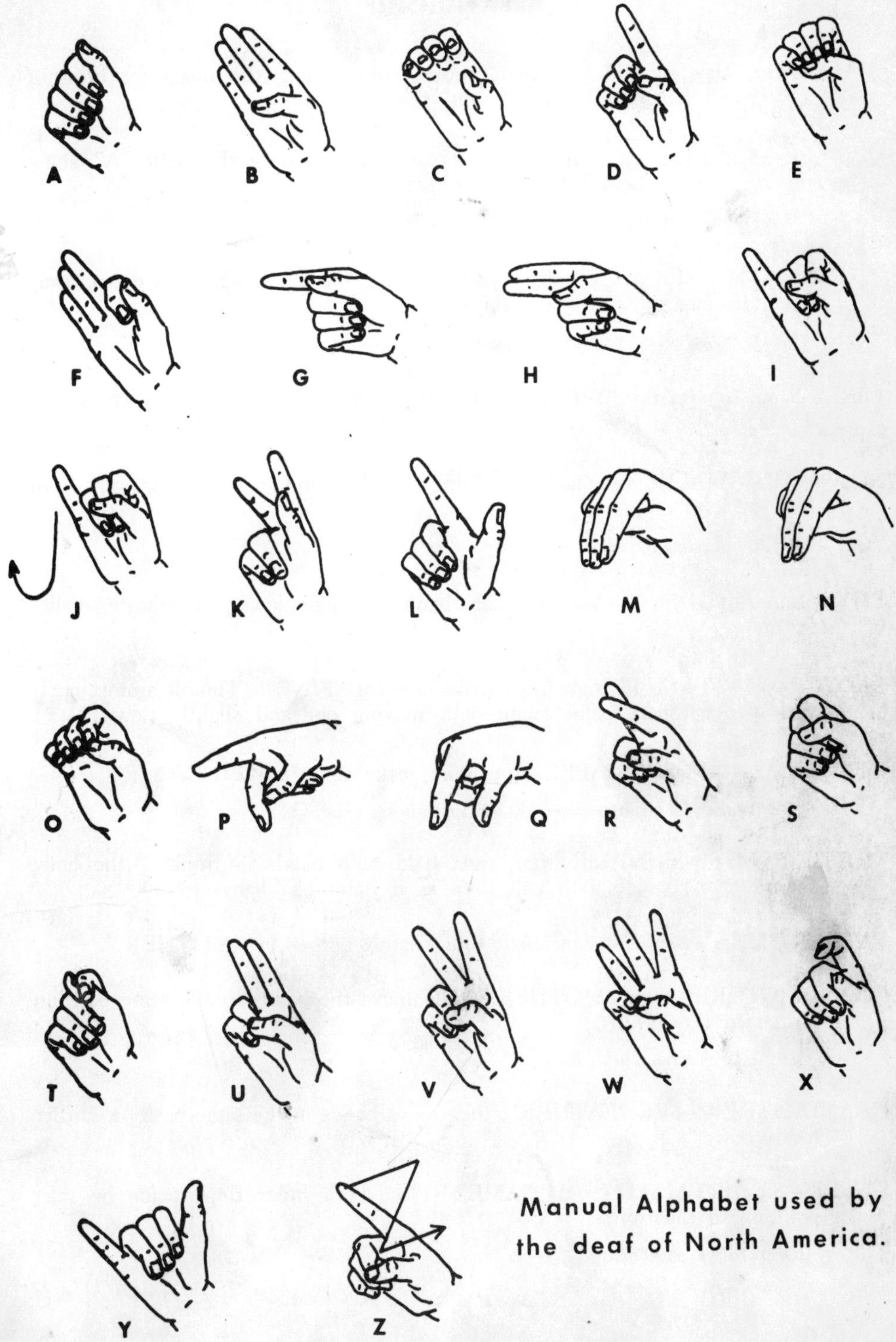

 F

 I

 J

 K

 L

 M

 N

 O

 P

 Q

 R

 S

T

U

V

W

X

 Y

Z

Manual Alphabet used by
the deaf of North America.

1

CHAPTER I

RELATIONSHIP

MALE—The basic sign for the male consists of grasping the imaginary brim of a hat with four fingers and thumb. (1)

FEMALE—The basic sign for the female consists of moving the right "A" along the right cheek toward the chin. (2)

> IDEA: Represents the old-fashioned bonnet string.

WOMAN—Make "FEMALE" sign and then bring the flat hand, palm down, away from the face at level of cheek. (3)

> IDEA: Indicating the height of the woman.

GIRL—Same sign as for "WOMAN" but the right hand is brought lower to indicate smaller stature.

MAN—Make "MALE" sign and then bring the flat hand, palm down, away from head at level of hat.

> IDEA: Indicating the height of the man.

BOY—Same sign as for "MAN" but right hand is brought lower, to indicate smaller stature.

LADY—Make "FEMALE" sign; then make sign for "FINE" (Thumb against chest with fingers open, palm facing left, moving out and slightly down). (4)

GENTLEMAN—Make "MALE" sign; then make sign for "FINE."

> IDEA: Man with a ruffle, as worn by gentlemen in years past.

MOTHER—Make "FEMALE" sign; then hold both hands in front of the body toward the left side with palms up as if holding a baby. (5)

FATHER—Make "MALE" sign; then bring hands out as in "MOTHER."

GRANDMOTHER—Sign "MOTHER"; then move the hands in the same position farther to the left. (6)

> IDEA: A generation farther back.

GRANDFATHER—Sign "FATHER"; then move hands in the same position farther to the left.

SISTER—Sign "FEMALE" and "SAME" (Place both index fingers side by side, pointing to the front). (7)

> IDEA: In the same family.

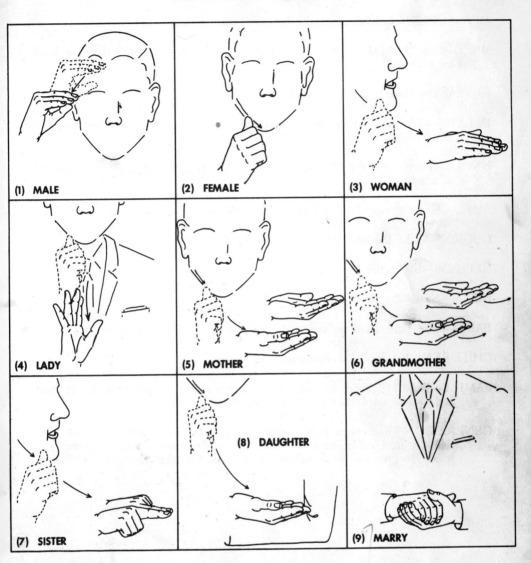

(1) MALE (2) FEMALE (3) WOMAN
(4) LADY (5) MOTHER (6) GRANDMOTHER
(7) SISTER (8) DAUGHTER (9) MARRY

Note: Refer to description for explanation and synonyms.

BROTHER—Make "MALE" sign; then make sign for "SAME."

DAUGHTER—Sign "FEMALE"; then place right hand in crook of left arm. (8)

SON—Make "MALE" sign; then place right hand in crook of left arm.

MARRY—Clasp the hands, with right hand on top. (9)

DIVORCE—Unclasp hands; or, slip imaginary ring off finger. (1).

WIFE—Sign "FEMALE"; then sign "MARRIED" (clasp hands with the right hand on top). (2)

HUSBAND—Make "MALE" sign; then sign "MARRIED."

IN-LAW—Make sign for the person and add "LAW" (right "L" against palm of left hand). (3)

UNCLE—Place the right "U" at the side of the temple and move it downward in a wavy motion. (4)

AUNT—Place the right "A" near the cheek and move it downward in a wavy motion.

COUSIN—Shake the letter "C" at side of cheek. (5)

NEPHEW—Shake the letter "N" at the side of temple. (6)

NIECE—Shake the letter "N" at side of chin.

BABY—Place right hand in crook of left arm as if rocking a baby. (7)

CHILDREN—Pat heads of imaginary children.

FAMILY—Place "F" hands in front of you, palms facing forward; draw hands apart and around until the little fingers are touching. (8)

GENERATION—Both open hands, palms facing back, come down from the right shoulder in a rolling motion. (This sign is sometimes made in reverse, i.e., hands progressing in a rolling motion toward the shoulder.) (9)

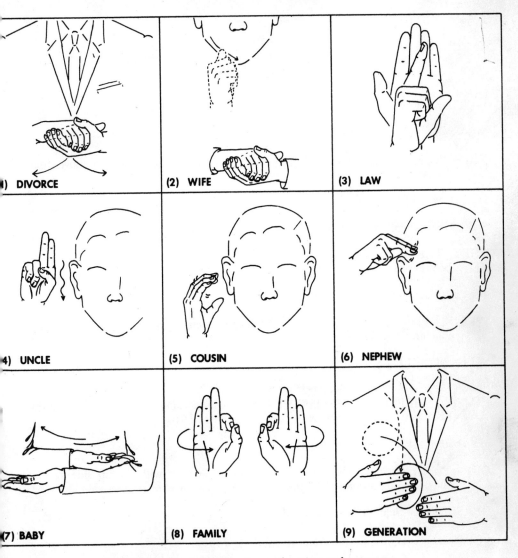

(1) DIVORCE   (2) WIFE   (3) LAW

(4) UNCLE   (5) COUSIN   (6) NEPHEW

(7) BABY   (8) FAMILY   (9) GENERATION

Note: Refer to description for explanation and synonyms.

CHAPTER II

PRONOUNS

I—"I" is placed at the chest. (1)

ME—Point right index finger at yourself.

YOU—Point index finger out. (For plural, point index finger out and move from left to right.)

HE, HIM—Sign "MALE" and point out with index finger.

SHE, HER—Sign "FEMALE" and point out with index finger.

THEY, THEM, THOSE, THESE—Point index finger at several imaginary objects before you. (2)

THAT—Place the right "Y" on left palm. (3)

WE, US—Place index finger at right shoulder and circle forward and around until touching the left shoulder. (4)

SELF, MYSELF—Strike "A" hand, palm facing left, against the chest, several times. (5)

HIMSELF, HERSELF, THEMSELVES, YOURSELF—Direct the "A" hand away from you in several short quick movements. (6)

MY, MINE—Place palm on chest. (7)

OUR—Place right hand, slightly cupped, at right shoulder with thumb side against body, circling around until the little finger side touches the left shoulder. (8)

OURSELVES—Sign "OUR" and "SELF."

YOUR—Face palm out, directing it forward. (9)

HIS, HER, THEIR—Face palm out, directing it toward the individuals. (Sometimes the "MALE" or "FEMALE" signs precede the sign for clarity.)

THINE (Deity)—Direct the open palm upward. (10)

THEE, THOU (Deity)—Point upward with index finger.

ALL—Face the left open hand toward the body; make a circle with the right hand, going out and around the left hand, ending with the back of the right hand in the palm of the left. (11)

EACH, EVERY—Hold up the left "A" and use the inside of the thumb of the right "A" to make downward strokes on the back of the left thumb. (12)

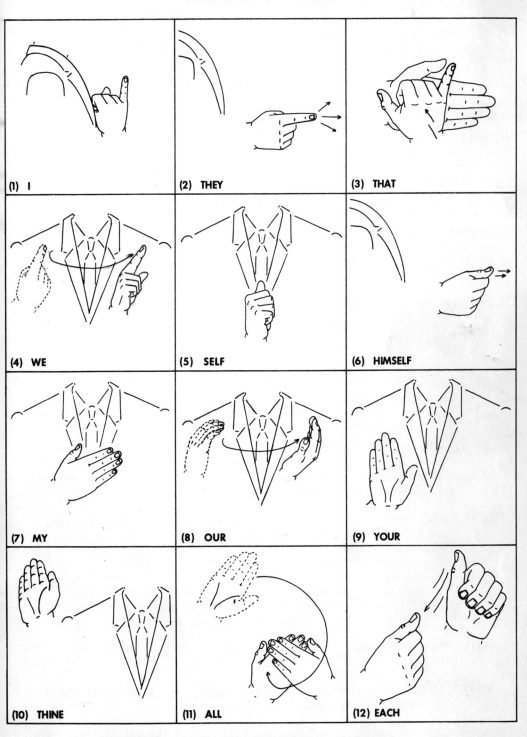

(1) I

(2) THEY

(3) THAT

(4) WE

(5) SELF

(6) HIMSELF

(7) MY

(8) OUR

(9) YOUR

(10) THINE

(11) ALL

(12) EACH

Note: Refer to description for explanation and synonyms.

ANY—Place the "A" hand before the body and draw it to the right while moving it up and down from the wrist so that the thumb points first up and then down. (1)

ANYONE—Sign "ANY" and "ONE."

EVERYBODY, EVERYONE—Sign "EACH" and "ONE."

WHATEVER, WHOEVER, WHOSOEVER—Make the sign for the desired pronoun and add "ANY."

ONE ANOTHER, EACH OTHER, FELLOWSHIP—Circle the right "A" (pointing down) in a counterclockwise motion around the thumb of the left "A" which is pointing up. (2)

OTHER, ANOTHER—Move the "A" hand slightly up and to the right. (3)

SOMEONE, SOMETHING—Hold up the right index finger and shake it back and forth slightly, left to right. (Palm side may face forward or self.) (4)

ANYTHING—Sign "ANY" and "THING" (Drop the slightly curved open hand before you, palm facing up; move it to the right and drop it again).

CHAPTER III

QUESTION WORDS

WHAT—Draw the right index downward across the left open palm. (5)

WHERE—Both open hands palms up, are circled outwardly (right hand clockwise and left hand counterclockwise). (6)

WHEN—Left index is held up facing you; right index faces out and describes a circle before the left index coming to rest on the tip of the left index. (7) This sign is sometimes made by pointing the index fingers forward with palms up and bringing them to the center ending with index fingers side by side (palms down). (8)

HOW—Place the curved hands back to back with fingers pointing down, turn hands in this position until the fingers point up. (9)

WHY—Touch the fingertips to the forehead and draw them away forming a "Y," palm facing self. (10)

WHICH—Place both "A" hands before you with palms facing each other and raise and lower them alternately. (11)

WHO—Describe a circle around the pursed lips toward the left with the index finger. (12)

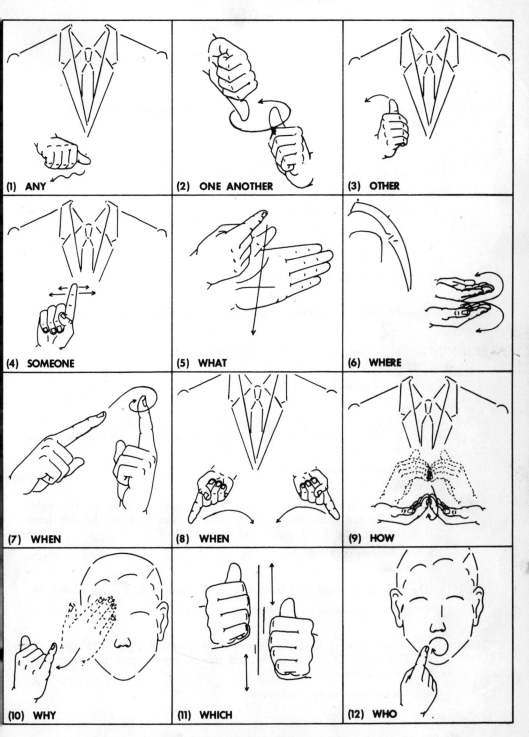

(1) ANY

(2) ONE ANOTHER

(3) OTHER

(4) SOMEONE

(5) WHAT

(6) WHERE

(7) WHEN

(8) WHEN

(9) HOW

(10) WHY

(11) WHICH

(12) WHO

Note: Refer to description for explanation and synonyms.

CHAPTER IV

TIME

TIME—Crook the index finger and tap the back of the left hand several times. (1)

> IDEA: *Indicates ticking of watch.*

TIME—Make a clockwise circle with the right "T" in the left palm. This sign is used in the abstract sense. (2)

DAY—The right arm, with index finger pointing out, palm up, is moved in an arc from right to left (or from left to right) while the fingertips of the left hand, palm down, are touching the right arm near the elbow. (3)

> IDEA: *Indicates the course of the sun.*

NOW—Place both bent hands before you at waist level, palms up. Drop hands slightly. (4)

> IDEA: *Indicates the time that is immediately before you.*

TODAY—Sign "NOW" and "DAY." (Sometimes the order is reversed.)

MORNING—The fingertips of the left hand are placed in the crook of the right arm; the right arm, with the palm up, moves upward. (5)

> IDEA: *Indicates the sun coming up.*

NOON—The fingertips of the left hand, palm down, touch the right arm near the elbow. The right arm is held straight up with the open palm facing to the left. (6)

> IDEA: *Indicates that the sun is overhead.*

AFTERNOON—The left arm is before you, palm down, pointing to the right. The right forearm, palm facing down, rests on the back of the left hand so that the arm and hand point slightly upward. (7)

> IDEA: *Indicates the sun halfway down.*

NIGHT—The wrist of the right bent hand rests on the back of the left open hand. (8)

> IDEA: *Indicates that the sun has gone down over the horizon.*

SUNRISE—The left arm is held before the body pointing right with the palm down. The right "O" starts below and moves upward past the outer edge of the left forearm. (9)

> IDEA: *The sun coming up over the horizon.*

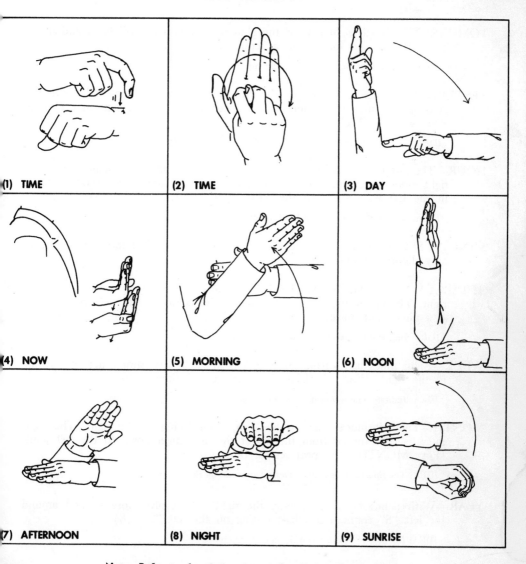

(1) TIME   (2) TIME   (3) DAY

(4) NOW   (5) MORNING   (6) NOON

(7) AFTERNOON   (8) NIGHT   (9) SUNRISE

Note: Refer to description for explanation and synonyms.

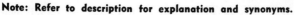

SUNSET—The left arm is held before the body pointing right with the palm down. The right "O" starts above and moves down past the outer edge of the left forearm.

    IDEA: The sun sinking below the horizon.

TOMORROW—Touch right side of the chin with thumb of "A" hand and direct it slightly up and forward in a semicircle. (1)

> IDEA: *Indicates the time which is before you.*

YESTERDAY—Touch right side of the chin with thumb of the "Y" hand and describe a semicircle up and back toward the ear. (This sign may also be made with the "A" hand.) (2)

> IDEA: *"Y" for yesterday moved back to represent time behind you.*

HOUR—The left hand is held before you, pointing up and palm facing right. The right index finger and thumb rest against the left hand and describe a circle in the left palm, twisting the wrist as the circle is made. (3)

> IDEA: *Indicating the moving of the hand of the clock.*

MINUTE, SECOND—Position is the same as for "HOUR" but index finger moves only slightly forward. (4)

AFTER A WHILE—The left hand is held before you pointing up with palm facing right. Thumb of the right "L" touches the center of the left palm acting as a pivot, and moves forward. (5)

> IDEA: *Indicates the passing of time on the clock.*

WEEK—Right index hand, palm down, is passed across left palm which is pointing to the right. (For "WEEKLY" repeat several times.) (6)

> IDEA: *Indicates one row of dates on the calendar.*

MONTH—The left index finger is held up, palm facing to the right. The right index is then moved from the tip of the left finger down to the last joint. (For "MONTHLY" repeat several times.) (7)

> IDEA: *The tip and three joints indicate four weeks on the calendar.*

YEAR—With palms facing the body, the right "S" revolves forward and around the left "S" coming to a halt resting on the left "S." (8)

> IDEA: *Indicates the earth revolving around the sun.*

FUTURE, BY AND BY, LATER—Raised arm with open right hand, palm toward cheek, moves upward and forward in a large semicircle. The larger and slower the sign is made, the greater the distance in the future is meant. (9)

PAST, WAS, WERE, AGO, LAST (PREVIOUS), FORMERLY—Open hand facing back moves backward over right shoulder. The larger and slower the sign is made the greater the distance in the past is meant. (10)

IS, AM, ARE—Place the tip of the index finger at the mouth; move it forward, still upright. (11)

DAILY—Place the "A" hand on the cheek near the chin and rub it forward several times. (12)

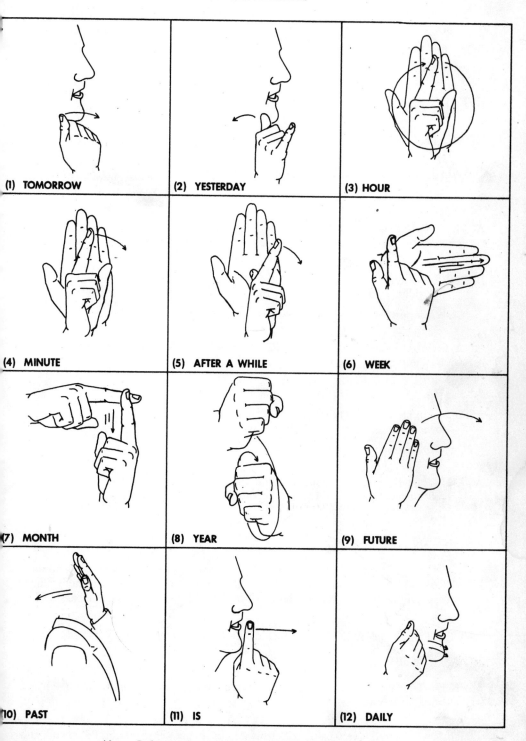

(1) TOMORROW

(2) YESTERDAY

(3) HOUR

(4) MINUTE

(5) AFTER A WHILE

(6) WEEK

(7) MONTH

(8) YEAR

(9) FUTURE

(10) PAST

(11) IS

(12) DAILY

Note: Refer to description for explanation and synonyms.

ALWAYS—Describe a clockwise circle before you with the index finger, palm facing up. (1)

> IDEA: *A circle is never ending.*

EVERLASTING, FOREVER—Sign "ALWAYS" and "STILL."

STILL, YET—Move the right "Y" hand forward, palm facing down. (2)

NEVER—Move the right open hand, palm down, in a circular movement before the body as follows: up-right-down-left; then move it off to the right. (3)

AFTER, ACROSS—The little finger edge of the right open hand passes across the back of the left open hand which is facing palm down. (4)

BEFORE—Open hands are back to back before you (right hand facing you) and the right is drawn away from the left towards the right shoulder. (5)

> IDEA: *Back over the shoulder always indicates the past.*

IN A FEW DAYS—Sign "TOMORROW" and "FEW" ("A" hand opens slowly as thumb passes along the opening fingers).

> IDEA: *A few tomorrows.*

A FEW DAYS AGO—Thumb of "A" hand touches right side of chin and opens toward the ear into the "FEW" sign.

> IDEA: *A few yesterdays.*

AGAIN—The right curved hand faces up then turns and moves to the left so that the finger tips touch the left open palm which is pointing forward with palm facing right. (6)

OFTEN—Sign "AGAIN" several times.

REGULAR—Place the little finger edge of the right "G" hand on the index finger edge of the left "G"; move both hands forward and strike together again. (7)

ONCE—Tip of the right index touches the center of the left palm and comes toward the body and up in a quick circular movement. (8)

TWICE—Touch the left palm with the middle finger of the right "2" hand and bring it toward you and up.

THRICE—Touch the left palm with the middle finger of the right "3" hand and bring it toward you and up.

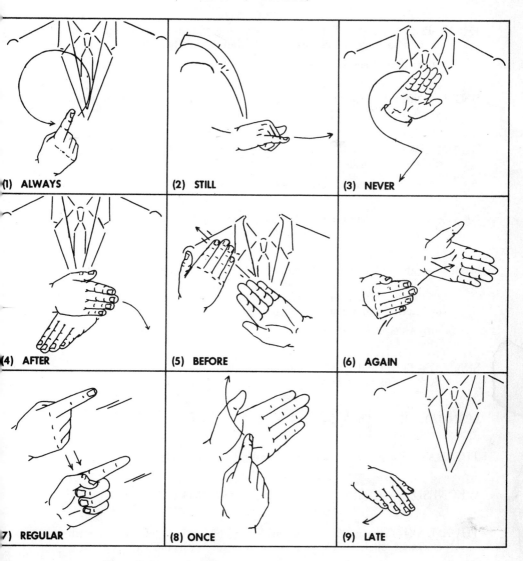

(1) ALWAYS

(2) STILL

(3) NEVER

(4) AFTER

(5) BEFORE

(6) AGAIN

(7) REGULAR

(8) ONCE

(9) LATE

Note: Refer to description for explanation and synonyms.

SOMETIMES, ONCE IN A WHILE—The sign for "ONCE" is repeated several
times.

LATE, NOT YET—Place the right hand near the hip with fingers pointing down
and palm facing the back. Hand is moved back and forth several times. (9)

IDEA: You are behind those who have already arrived.

THEN—Place the left "L" before you with the thumb pointing up; then with the right index finger touch first the left thumb and then the left index finger. (1)

> IDEA: Thumb indicates "first" and then comes the next finger.

UNTIL—Direct the right index finger in a forward arc and touch the left index which is pointing up. (2)

DURING, WHILE—Both index fingers, palms down and pointing forward, separated slightly, are pushed slightly down and then forward. (3)

> IDEA: Hands moving forward show time going on.

NEXT—Left open hand faces the body; the right open hand is placed between the left hand and the body and then passes over the left. (4)

SINCE—Right index finger at right shoulder points forward toward the left; place left index finger in front of it also pointing toward the left. Both index fingers are circled under-back-up-forward ending with both index fingers facing up, right hand behind the left. (5)

> IDEA: From the past to the present.

SUNDAY—Both hands are held before the body, fingers pointing up and palms out. Both hands are moved in opposite circular motions. (6)

MONDAY—Right "M" describes a small clockwise circle. (7)

TUESDAY—Right "T" describes a small clockwise circle.

WEDNESDAY—Right "W" describes a small clockwise circle.

THURSDAY—Form a "T," then quickly change to an "H" and describe a small clockwise circle. This sign is often made with the "H" only.

FRIDAY—Right "F" describes a small clockwise circle.

SATURDAY—Right "S" describes a small clockwise circle.

SPRING, GROW—The right "AND" hand opens as it comes up through the left "C" which is held before you with the palm facing right. (8)

> IDEA: Right hand indicates that which is coming up out of the ground.

SUMMER—The right index finger is crooked and wiped across the forehead.

> IDEA: Wiping off perspiration.

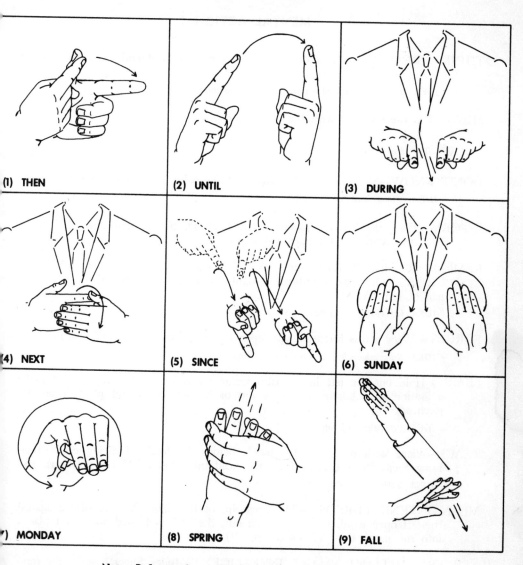

(1) THEN	(2) UNTIL	(3) DURING
(4) NEXT	(5) SINCE	(6) SUNDAY
(7) MONDAY	(8) SPRING	(9) FALL

Note: Refer to description for explanation and synonyms.

FALL—The left open hand points upward toward the right. The right open hand brushes downward along the left forearm with the edge of the right index. (9)

   IDEA: Leaves falling off a tree.

WINTER, COLD, CHILLY—Shake both "S" hands, palms facing each other.

   IDEA: Shivering from the cold.

CHAPTER V

MENTAL ACTION

THINK, MEDITATE—The index finger faces the forehead and describes a small circle. (1)
> IDEA: Indicates something is going around in the mind.

MIND—Tap the forehead with the curved index finger. (2)

KNOW—Pat forehead. (3)

DON'T KNOW—Sign "KNOW" and turn the palm out away from the head.
> IDEA: "Know" and "not."

INFORM—Place the "AND" hands at the forehead; move them down and away from you, ending with open palms up. (4)

REMEMBER—Sign "KNOW" and "STAY" (place right "A" on thumbnail of left "A"). Or, place thumbnail of right "A" on forehead and then on thumbnail of left "A." (5)
> IDEA: Knowledge which stays.

FORGET—Wipe across forehead with open hand, ending in the "A" position. (6)
> IDEA: Knowledge which is wiped off the mind.

LEARN—Hold out the left hand, palm facing up and with the right hand make a motion as if taking something out of the left hand and place it on the forehead. (7)
> IDEA: From the book into the mind.

TEACH—Place both open "AND" hands before the forehead facing each other; bring them forward, away from the head into closed "AND" positions. (8)
> IDEA: Taking something from your mind.

MEAN, INTEND, PURPOSE—The fingertips of the right "V" are placed against the left open hand, the "V" facing out; the "V" is turned and again placed into the palm, the "V" facing in. (9)

CLEVER, BRILLIANT, SMART, INTELLIGENT—Index finger touches the forehead and moves upward with a shaking motion. (10)
> IDEA: The mind has brilliance, indicated by the scintillating motion of the finger.

WISE—Crook the right index finger and move it up and down in front of the forehead, palm facing down. (11)
> IDEA: Indicating the depth of knowledge in the mind.

STUPID—Strike "A" hand against forehead several times, palm facing in. (12)
> IDEA: Thick skull, hard to penetrate.

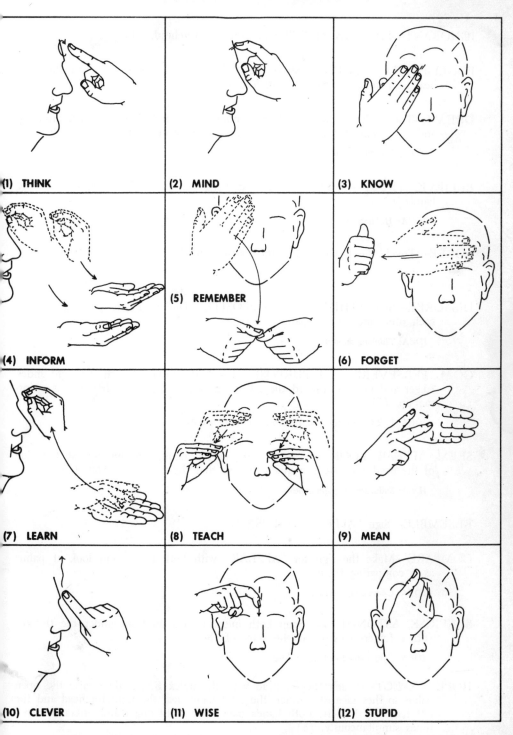

(1) THINK

(2) MIND

(3) KNOW

(4) INFORM

(5) REMEMBER

(6) FORGET

(7) LEARN

(8) TEACH

(9) MEAN

(10) CLEVER

(11) WISE

(12) STUPID

Note: Refer to description for explanation and synonyms.

IGNORANT—Place back of "V" hand on the forehead. (1)

FOOLISH, SILLY, ABSURD—Shake the "Y" hand back and forth before the forehead several times, palm facing left. (2)

DREAM—Touch the forehead with the index finger and draw it away, crooking and uncrooking the finger several times, palm facing you. (3)

  IDEA: *The mind going off into fantasies.*

BELIEVE, TRUST—Touch the forehead with the index finger and clasp the hands. (4)

  IDEA: *Holding on to the thought.*

AGREE—Touch the forehead and then sign "SAME."

  IDEA: *Thinking the same.*

DISAGREE—Sign "THINK" and "OPPOSITE" (index fingers pointing toward each other are pulled apart).

  IDEA: *Thinking opposite.*

GOAL, PERSEVERE, AIM, PURPOSE—Touch the forehead with the right index finger and move it toward the left index which is held higher and is pointing up. (5)

  IDEA: *Left hand is the goal, right hand works toward it.*

SEEM, APPEAR, LOOK—Place the right curved hand, pointing up, at the side of the head and give it a quick turn so that the palm faces you. (6)

  IDEA: *Suddenly the palm appears.*

RESEMBLE—Sign "APPEAR" and "SAME."

COMPARE—Make the sign for "APPEAR" with both hands and look at palms as if comparing them.

  IDEA: *Comparing the palms.*

SURPRISE, ASTONISHED—Snap both index fingers up from under the thumbs (other fingers closed) at the sides of the eyes. (7)

  IDEA: *Eyes opened wide in surprise.*

HOPE, EXPECT—Touch the forehead with the index finger; then raise the open palms so they face each other, the right hand near the right forehead and the left hand at the left. Both hands bend to a right angle and unbend several times simultaneously. (8)

  IDEA: *Thinking and beckoning for something to come.*

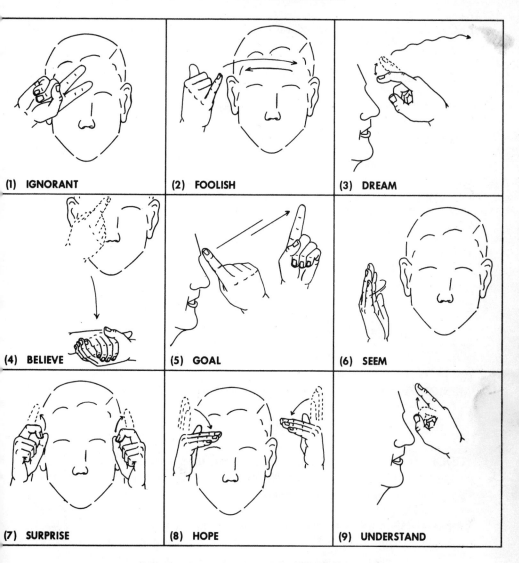

(1) IGNORANT	(2) FOOLISH	(3) DREAM
(4) BELIEVE	(5) GOAL	(6) SEEM
(7) SURPRISE	(8) HOPE	(9) UNDERSTAND

Note: Refer to description for explanation and synonyms.

UNDERSTAND—Place the "S" hand before the forehead, palm facing self, and snap the index finger up. (9)

> IDEA: *Suddenly the light goes on.*

MISUNDERSTAND—Touch forehead with index finger of "V" hand and then with middle finger of the "V" hand.

> IDEA: *The thought is turned around.*

BECAUSE—Touch the forehead with the index finger of the "L" hand; then draw it slightly up and to the right forming an "A." (1)

FOR—Point toward the right side of the forehead with index finger; then circle downward and forward ending with the index finger pointing forward at eye level. (2)

REASON—"R" hand revolves before the forehead.

> IDEA: *Making the "think" sign with an "R."*

WONDER—Point the index finger toward the forehead and revolve it slowly as in "THINK." (Or, revolve the right "W.")

IDEA—Touch the forehead with the tip of the "I" hand and turn it so the palm faces out. (3)

> IDEA: *A little thought comes forward.*

IMAGINATION—Place the "I" hand so that it faces the forehead; then circle it upward and away from the head two or three times. (4)

> IDEA: *Thoughts circling around.*

MEMORIZE—Touch the forehead with the index finger; then draw away into an "S." (5)

> IDEA: *The thought is firmly grasped.*

JUDGE—Touch the forehead with index finger; then move both "F" hands up and down alternately (palms facing each other and fingers pointing forward). (6)

> IDEA: *Thoughts are being weighed in the balance.*

DECIDE, DETERMINE, RESOLVE—Touch the forehead with index finger; then drop both hands before you into an "F," palms facing each other.

> IDEA: *You have weighed the thoughts and have come to a decision.*

IF—Place the "F" hands before you, tips pointing forward and palms facing each other; raise and lower them alternately. (Same sign as "JUDGE" except that the up and down movement is shorter.)

OR, EITHER—Sign "WHICH."

ATTENTION, CONCENTRATION—Place open hands at either side of the eyes, like blinders on a horse; then move both hands forward. (7)

> IDEA: *Blinders help one to concentrate and prevent one from looking to the right or the left.*

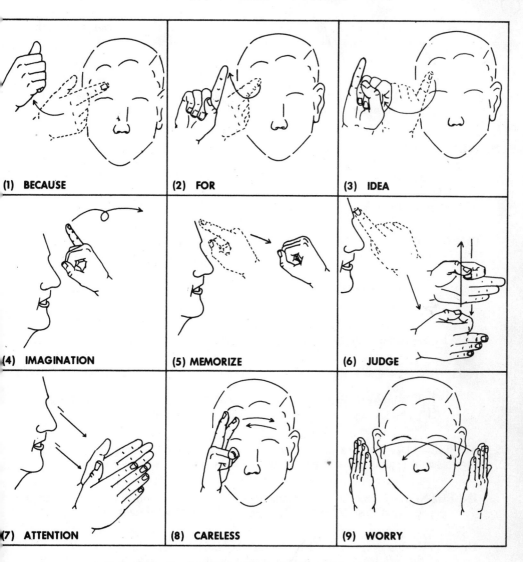

(1) BECAUSE (2) FOR (3) IDEA

(4) IMAGINATION (5) MEMORIZE (6) JUDGE

(7) ATTENTION (8) CARELESS (9) WORRY

Note: Refer to description for explanation and synonyms.

CARELESS—Pass the "V" hand back and forth before the forehead, palm facing to the left. (8)

WORRY, TROUBLE—Right open hand, palm facing left, passes before the face and down toward the left shoulder. Same motion is made alternately with the left hand several times. (9)

IDEA: *Everything is coming at you.*

SUSPECT—Crook and uncrook the index finger before the forehead several times (palm facing self). (1)

> IDEA: Question in the mind.

OBEY—Both "A" hands, with palms facing the body, are dropped from eye-level, opening into bent positions, facing up. (2)

> IDEA: Hands coming down in obedience.

DISOBEY—Both "A" hands are before the face at eye level and then make a quick turn outward so that they face forward. (This sign is sometimes made with only one hand.) (3)

> IDEA: Hands refusing to come down in obedience.

DOUBT—Place the "A" hands before the face, palms facing forward and move them up and down alternately. (4)

HONOR—Bring the "H" hand toward the face and down, ending with the "H" fingers pointing up. (5)

RESPECT—Same sign as "HONOR" made with the letter "R."

NOT, DON'T—Cross the open hands before you, palms down, and draw them apart. (6)
Or, more informally, "NOT" is signed by placing the thumb of the right "A" hand under the chin and directing it forward. (7)

ADVISE—Place the tips of the right "AND" hand on the back of the left open hand (palms down) and open the right as it is moved forward.

INFLUENCE—Place the tips of the right "AND" hand on the back of the left open hand (as "ADVISE"); then circle left-forward-right. (8)

DECEIVE—Place the right "Y" (with the index finger extended) on the back of the left hand which is in a similar position and slide it forward lengthwise across the back of the left. (9)

INDIFFERENT, DOESN'T MATTER—Brush the tips of both open hands up and down several times, palms facing up. (10)

EXPERIENCE—Grasp the lower edge of the left open hand with the right tips which are closed against the palm, and pull away. (11)

PROOF—Touch the mouth with the index finger; then place back of the right open hand in left palm. (12)

> IDEA: Place it where one can see it.

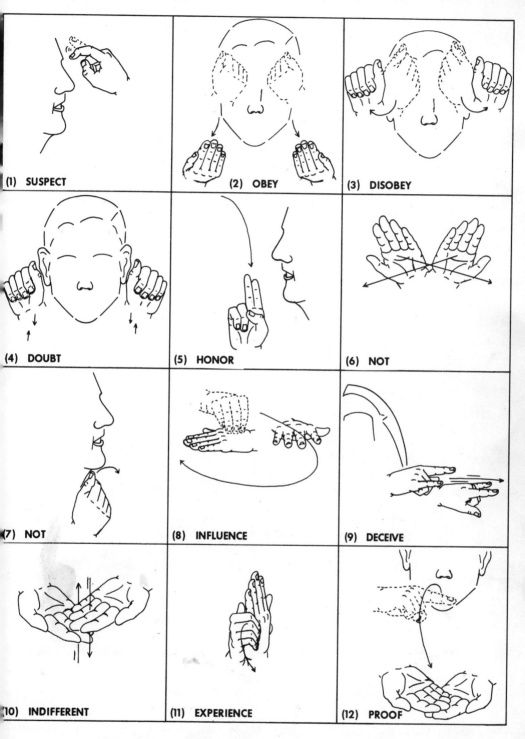

(1) SUSPECT

(2) OBEY

(3) DISOBEY

(4) DOUBT

(5) HONOR

(6) NOT

(7) NOT

(8) INFLUENCE

(9) DECEIVE

(10) INDIFFERENT

(11) EXPERIENCE

(12) PROOF

Note: Refer to description for explanation and synonyms.

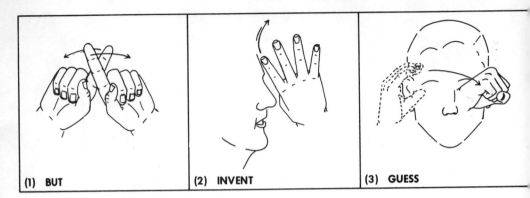

(1) BUT (2) INVENT (3) GUESS

Note: Refer to description for explanation and synonyms.

BUT—Cross the index fingers, palms facing out, and draw them apart. (1)

DON'T CARE—Place the tips of the right "AND" hand on the forehead and open it as you turn it and throw it forward.

HABIT—Sign "MIND" and "BOUND."

INVENT—The "4" hand, index finger touching the center of the forehead, pushes upward the full length of the forefinger. (2)

GUESS—Place the right "C" hand near the right side of the forehead and pass the hand before the face ending with the "S" position. (3)

STUBBORN—Place the thumb of the right open hand against the side of the head, palm facing forward, and bend the hand forward.

> IDEA: Like a mule.

CRAZY—Point the right index finger toward the forehead and circle several times, palm facing self.

> IDEA: Wheels in the head.

DIZZY—Place the bent "five" hand before the forehead, palm facing in, and circle several times.

CHAPTER VI

EMOTION AND FEELING

LOVE—Closed or open hands crossed and pressed to the heart. (1)
>   IDEA: *Pressing to one's heart.*

HATE, DISLIKE—Both open hands pointing up, palms out, are pushed away from the body toward the right side, the right hand in front of the left. (This sign may also be made by snapping the middle finger from under the thumb as the hands are pushed away). (2)
>   IDEA: *The object is pushed away from you.*

HAPPY, GLAD, REJOICE, JOY—The open hands pat the chest several times with a slight upward motion. (3)
>   IDEA: *Patting the chest indicates happiness.*

SAD, DEJECTED—Hold both open hands before the face, fingers slightly apart and pointing up; then drop both hands a short distance and bend the head slightly (4)
>   IDEA: *Long-faced, gloomy.*

CROSS, GROUCHY—The curved hand, with fingers slightly separated, is bent and unbent several times before the face (palm in). (5)
>   IDEA: *The face is twisted.*

ANGRY—Place the curved "5" hands against the waist and draw up against the sides of the body. (6)
>   IDEA: *Tearing the clothes in anger.*

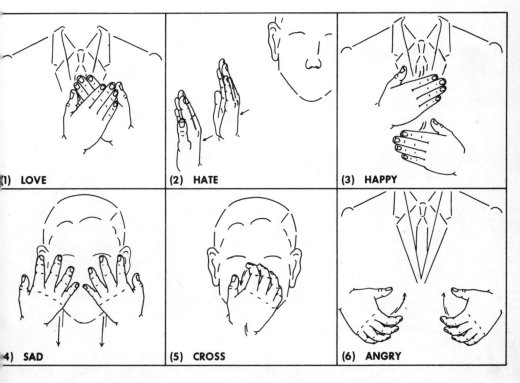

(1) LOVE   (2) HATE   (3) HAPPY

(4) SAD   (5) CROSS   (6) ANGRY

Note: Refer to description for explanation and synonyms.

SORRY—Rub the "A" hand in a circular motion over the heart. (1)

LAUGH, CHEERFUL, SMILE—Place index fingers at the corners of mouth and draw them upward several times. (For "SMILE" the sign is sometimes made with the "4" hands drawn from the sides of the mouth across the cheeks. (2)
IDEA: Corners of the mouth turned up.

CRY—Draw the index fingers down the cheeks from the eyes several times.
IDEA: Tears coursing down the cheeks.

KISS—Place the tips of the "AND" hand at the mouth and then on the cheek.

SATISFY, CONTENT—Both open hands, palms down, are placed against the chest, right above the left, and pushed down. (3)
IDEA: The inner feelings are quieted.

DISCONTENT, COMPLAIN, DISSATISFIED—The curved "5" hand is placed on the chest and then the arm and hand are moved back and forth slightly but the fingers remain against the chest. (4)
IDEA: The inner feelings are stirred.

PEACE—Right palm is placed on left palm and then turned so the left palm is on top; then both hands palms down, move down and toward the sides. (5)

COMFORTABLE, COMFORT—Using curved hands, stroke forward first on the back of the left and then on the back of the right hand.

CONFUSION, MIXED UP—The left curved "5" is held before you, palm facing up; the right curved "5," palm down, circles counterclockwise above it. (6)

KIND, GRACIOUS—The open hand is placed on the body over the heart and is then moved up-out-down-in-up around the left open hand which faces the body pointing to the right. (7)
IDEA: As if winding a bandage.

MEAN—The knuckles of the bent right middle and index fingers strike the knuckles of the left bent middle and index fingers in a sharp downward stroke (palms facing self). (8)

REVENGE—Join the index finger and thumb tips of each hand and strike the tips together several times.

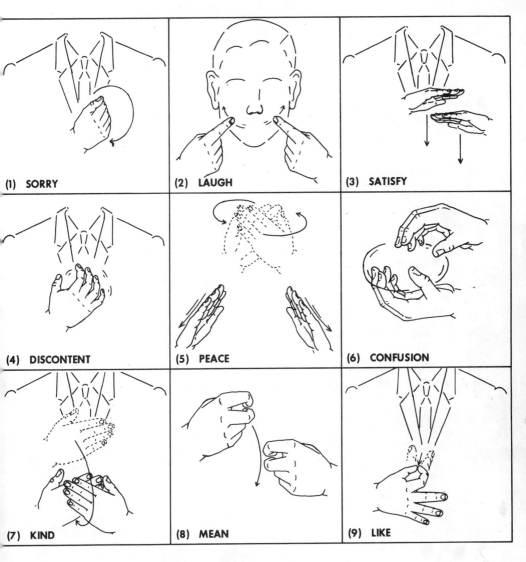

(1) SORRY

(2) LAUGH

(3) SATISFY

(4) DISCONTENT

(5) PEACE

(6) CONFUSION

(7) KIND

(8) MEAN

(9) LIKE

Note: Refer to description for explanation and synonyms.

CRUEL, RUDE—Strike the side of the right index hand against the left index and forward.

LIKE—Place the thumb and forefinger against the chest (other fingers separated) and draw them away from the body, closing the two fingers, palm still facing the body. (9)

    IDEA: Indicating the heart is drawn toward the object.

PLEASE, PLEASURE, ENJOY (also used for LIKE)—Rub the open hand on the chest in a circular motion. (1)

> IDEA: Rubbing the heart to indicate pleasure.

WANT, DESIRE, WISH—Place both curved "5" hands before you, palms up, and draw them toward you several times. (2)

> IDEA: Drawing an object toward one's self.

DON'T WANT—Sign "WANT" and then turn the hands over in this position, ending with palms facing down.

SELFISH—Point the "V" hands forward (palms down) and draw them back towards self, crooking the fingers. (3)

> IDEA: Drawing everything toward one's self.

FEEL—Place the tip of the middle finger against the chest, with other fingers extended; draw it up a short distance. (4)

> IDEA: The finger feels the heart.

MERCY, PITY—Sign "FEEL" and still using the middle finger, stroke an imaginary person before you. (This sign is often made with both hands.) (5)

SYMPATHY—Sign "FEEL" and "WITH."

EXCITED, THRILLED—Alternately brush the middle finger tips of the "5" hands upward on the chest several times. (6)

> IDEA: The feelings are stirred.

JEALOUS, ENVIOUS—Bite the index finger; or, place the "J" finger in the corner of the mouth and twist it.

HUMBLE, MEEK—Right "B" is placed against the lips, palm facing left, and is then passed down and under the left hand which is open with palm facing down. (7)

> IDEA: One is willing to be under authority.

PROUD—Place the "A" hand against the chest and move it up slowly. (8)

> IDEA: Inner feelings rise.

BOAST—Place the "A" hand against the chest and push up against the chest in several short, quick movements.

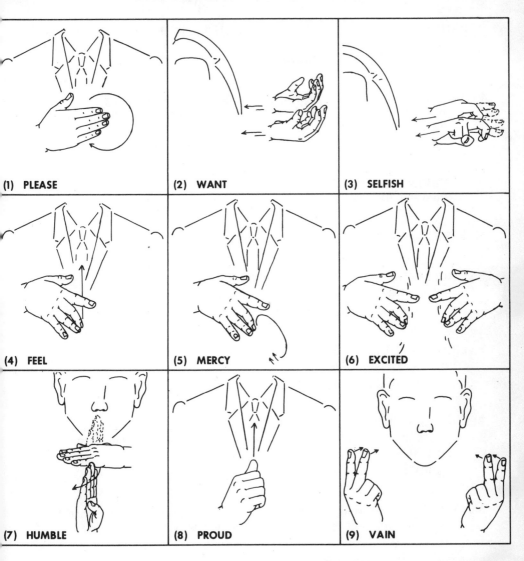

(1) PLEASE   (2) WANT   (3) SELFISH

(4) FEEL   (5) MERCY   (6) EXCITED

(7) HUMBLE   (8) PROUD   (9) VAIN

Note: Refer to description for explanation and synonyms.

EGOTISM—Sign "SELF."

VAIN, VANITY—Place the "V" hands before you, palms facing self, and move the "V" fingers up and down simultaneously. (9)

IDEA: All eyes looking at me.

AFRAID, SCARED—Hold both "AND" hands before the chest, fingers pointing toward each other; then open both hands and move the right hand toward the left and left hand toward the right, palms facing self. (1)

FEAR—Both "5" hands are held up at the left side, palms facing out, with the right hand behind the left. Draw both hands towards self with a slight shaking motion from the wrist. (2)

> IDEA: Hands held up to ward off danger.

AWKWARD—Place the "3" hands before you (palms down) and move them forward and back alternately.

NERVOUS—Place the "5" hands before you (palms down) and shake them slightly.

ENTHUSIASTIC, ZEALOUS, INDUSTRIOUS—Flat hands, palm to palm, are rubbed together.

> IDEA: Natural motion indicating enthusiasm.

PATIENT, ENDURE—Place the thumbnail of the right "A" against the lips and draw downward. (3)

> IDEA: Closing the mouth in suffering.

BLUSH—Sign "RED" (brush index finger down across lips); then place the "AND" hands, palms toward the face, at the sides of the cheeks and open hands as they move upward.

> IDEA: Face becoming red.

ASHAMED—Curved hand is placed against the cheek, palm down, and then turned, back of hand still against cheek, until the palm faces back. (4)

EMBARRASSED, BASHFUL, SHY—Slightly curved hands, with fingers slightly separated, face the cheeks and move upward with a shaking motion. (5)

> IDEA: Wanting to hide the face with the hands to cover confusion.

SUFFER—The right "S" revolves forward and around the left "S," both palms facing self. (6)

GRIEF—Place the "A" hands together, palm to palm and twist them.

> IDEA: The heart is crushed.

PAIN—The index fingers are jabbed toward each other several times. (7)

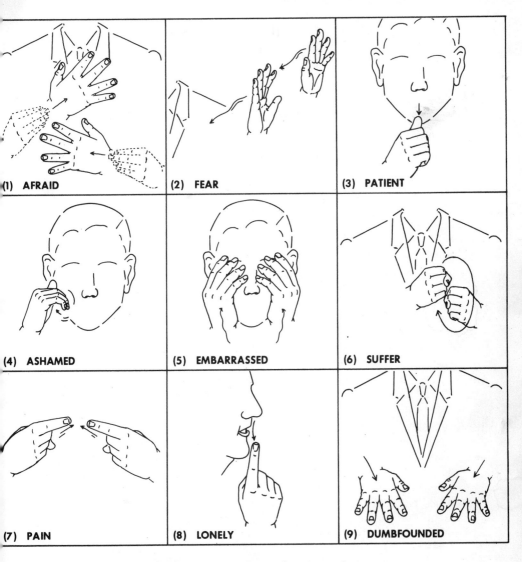

(1) AFRAID (2) FEAR (3) PATIENT

(4) ASHAMED (5) EMBARRASSED (6) SUFFER

(7) PAIN (8) LONELY (9) DUMBFOUNDED

Note: Refer to description for explanation and synonyms.

DISCOURAGED, DESPAIR—Touch the forehead with the index finger and then sign "FAIL."

LONELY, LONESOME—Draw the index finger down across the lips, palm facing left. (8)

DUMBFOUNDED, SHOCKED—Both open "5" hands, palms facing down, are pushed slightly forward while the body suddenly straightens up. (9)

CHAPTER VII

LOCATION

WITH—Place the "A" hands together, palm to palm. (1)

WITHOUT—Sign "WITH" and then open the hands as they are separated.

TOGETHER—Place the "A" hands together, palm to palm, and move them right-forward-left in a semicircle.

SEPARATE—Both curved hands with fingers back to back palms down, are pulled apart. (2)
> IDEA: That which has been together is separated.

UP—Point up with the index finger.

DOWN—Point down with the index finger.

ABOVE, OVER—Hold the right open hand above the left open hand, both palms down; move the right in a counterclockwise circle. (3)

BELOW, BENEATH, UNDER—Hold the right open hand under the left open hand, both palms down; move the right in a counterclockwise circle. (This sign is sometimes made as above using the right "A" with thumb pointing up.) (4)

FAR—Place both "A" hands before you, thumbs up, knuckles touching; move the right "A" forward. (When a great distance is indicated, the right moves forward with more effort.) (5)
> IDEA: Indicates distance from starting point.

NEAR, CLOSE TO, APPROACH—The back of the right bent hand approaches the inside of the left bent hand, both palms facing the body. (6)
> IDEA: One hand close to the other.

ON—Palm of the right open hand is placed on the back of the left open hand, both palms down. (7)
> IDEA: One hand on top of the other.

HERE—With both open hands, palms up, fingers pointing forward, describe circles, the right hand going to the right and the left hand going to the left. (8)
> IDEA: Indicates that which is before you.

34

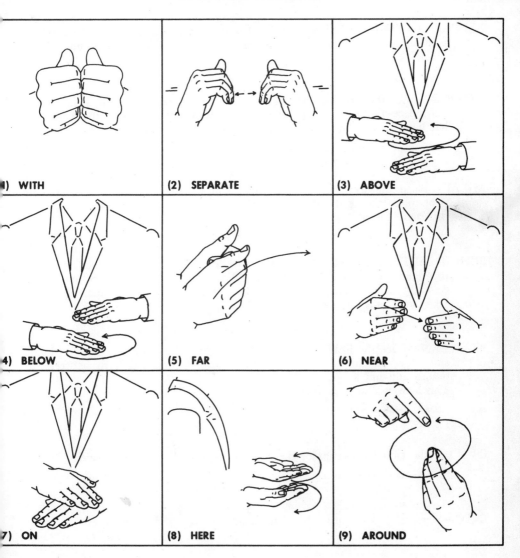

(1) WITH	(2) SEPARATE	(3) ABOVE
(4) BELOW	(5) FAR	(6) NEAR
(7) ON	(8) HERE	(9) AROUND

Note: Refer to description for explanation and synonyms.

THERE—Point out with the index finger if referring to a particular location. When used rather vaguely, circle the upturned open palm slightly toward the right.

AROUND—With the index finger, describe a counterclockwise circle around the upturned tips of the left "AND" hand. (9)

BEFORE, IN THE PRESENCE OF—The left open hand is held up, fingers pointing up and palm facing in; the right open hand moves up to face the left. (1)

BEYOND—Place the left open hand before you, fingers pointing right, palm toward self; place the right open hand, palm toward self, between the body and left hand, pass it over the left, down and forward. (2)

> IDEA: On the other side and a little distance farther.

AHEAD—Place the left hand before you, palm facing self and fingers pointing right; place the right palm against the back of the left hand and then move the right forward, away from the left.

BEHIND, AFTER—Place the "A" hands close together facing each other and move the right "A" behind the left "A." (To indicate that one is behind in accomplishment, place the right "A" behind the left "A" and draw the right "A" back some distance.) (3)

BETWEEN—Place the little finger side of the right open hand between the thumb and fingers of the left open hand and move it back and forth between the thumb and index finger. (4)
This sign is also used for "MEDIUM."

> IDEA: Between the thumb and fingers.

IN—Place the closed fingertips of the right hand into the left "C" hand. (5)

> IDEA: Placing something into the left hand.

INTO—Sign "IN" and push the right hand through and forward.

OUT—The right open "AND" hand, facing the body and pointing down becomes a closed "AND" as it is drawn up through the left "C" which then becomes an "O." (6)

> IDEA: Out of the left hand.

GONE—The right open "AND" hand facing the body and pointing up, becomes a closed "AND" as it is drawn down through the left "C" which then becomes an "O." (7)

OF—Spell, or use the possessive sign (open palm facing out); or use the sign for "JOIN" (linking together index and thumbs of both hands).

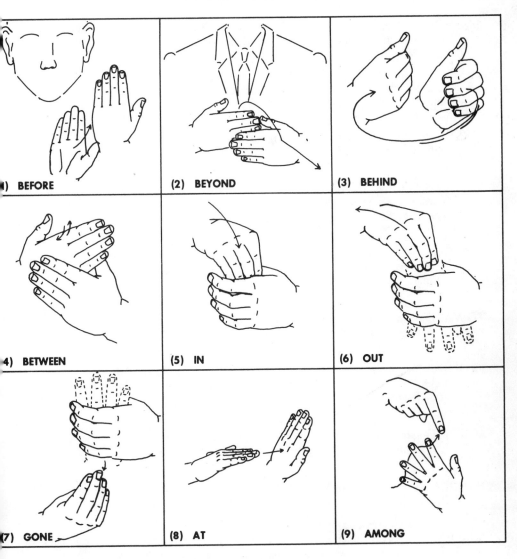

(1) BEFORE **(2) BEYOND** **(3) BEHIND**

(4) BETWEEN **(5) IN** **(6) OUT**

(7) GONE **(8) AT** **(9) AMONG**

Note: Refer to description for explanation and synonyms.

AT—Hold the left "B" hand before you, palm out; strike the back of the left with the tips of the right "B" hand, both hands pointing upward. (8)

AMONG—Hold up left "5" hand and pass the right index finger in and out between the fingers of the left hand. (9)

DISAPPEAR, VANISH—Hold up both open "AND" hands, palms facing self and tips pointing up; as the hands are drawn apart to the sides pass the thumb along the fingertips, ending with an "A" position in each hand. (1)

CENTER, MIDDLE—Describe a circle over the left palm with the right bent hand and then place the right fingertips in the center of the left palm.

FIRST—Hold up the left "A" hand with the thumb pointing up and strike it with the tip of the right index finger. (2)

LAST, END—Hold up the left "S" with the little finger extended; with a downward motion strike the end of the little finger with the right index finger (or little finger). (3)

TO—Direct the right index finger toward, and then touch, the left index fingertip which is pointing up. (The sign for "TO" is omitted in the infinitive form.) (4)

TOWARD—Direct the right index finger toward the left index finger tip which is pointing up, but do not touch it.

FROM—Point the left index finger to the right, palm facing in; then place the right "X," palm facing left, against the left index and pull it toward you and down. (5)

AGAINST—Strike the tips of the right open hand, palm facing self, against the left palm which is facing to the right.

THROUGH—Move the right open hand forward between the index and middle fingers of the left hand which is facing you. (6)

ACROSS—The little finger edge of the right open hand passes across the back of the left open hand which is facing palm down. (See illustration for "AFTER.")

ONWARD, FORWARD, PROGRESS—Both bent hands, tips pointing toward each other and palms facing self are moved away from the body. (7)

HIGH, ADVANCED—Both bent hands, tips pointing toward each other and palms facing down, are moved upward in stages. (The sign for "High" may also be made by moving the right index upward with a scintillating motion.) (8)

LEFT—Direct the "L" hand toward the left.

RIGHT—Direct the "R" hand toward the right.

LOCATION (continued)

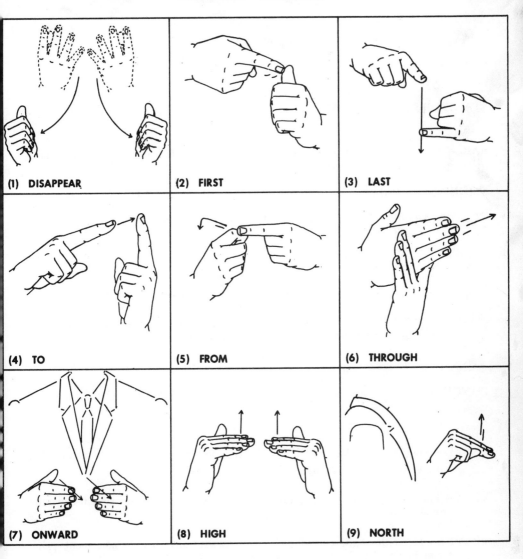

(1) DISAPPEAR	**(2) FIRST**	**(3) LAST**
(4) TO	**(5) FROM**	**(6) THROUGH**
(7) ONWARD	**(8) HIGH**	**(9) NORTH**

Note: Refer to description for explanation and synonyms.

NORTH—Direct the "N" hand up. (9)

SOUTH—Direct the "S" hand down.

EAST—Direct the "E" hand toward the right.

WEST—Direct the "W" hand toward the left.

> (When giving directions, it is often better to use the above initial signs in the actual direction of the compass.)

CHAPTER VIII

VERBS

STAND—Place the right "V" in a standing position on the left palm. (1)
>IDEA: *The two fingers represent the legs standing.*

FALL—Place the "V" in a standing position on the left palm, let the "V" fall, palm up, into the left hand. (2)

SLIDE—Sign "FALL" and slide the "V" forward on the left palm.

GET UP, ARISE, RESURRECTION—The right "V" with fingers pointing up and facing self is raised and then placed in a standing position on the left palm. (3)
>IDEA: *Rising from a reclining position to a standing position.*

LIE, RECLINE—Place the back of the right "V" hand in the left palm. (4)

JUMP—Place the right "V" in a standing position on the left palm; lift the "V," bending the knuckles and return to standing position. Repeat several times. (5)
>IDEA: *Bending the knees in jumping.*

DANCE, PARTY—Place the right "V" in a standing position on the left palm and swing the "V" back and forth. (6)
>IDEA: *The motion of dancing.*

KNEEL—Bend the knuckles of the right "V" and place in the left palm. (7)
>IDEA: *Fingers are in a kneeling position.*

VISIT—The "V" hands, pointing up and facing self, are rotated up-out-down-in-around each other. (8)

TRAVEL—Move the right curved "V" hand forward in a zigzag movement palm facing down. (9)

WALK—Open hands, palms down, are moved in a forward-downward motion alternately. (10)
>IDEA: *Representing feet walking.*

MARCH—Place both bent hands before you, fingers separated and palms facing down, right behind the left; swing the fingers back and forth as both hands move forward. (11)
>IDEA: *Indicating rows of soldiers marching.*

RUN—The right open palm facing up brushes outward to the right from under the left open palm. (12)
>IDEA: *A swift movement away.*

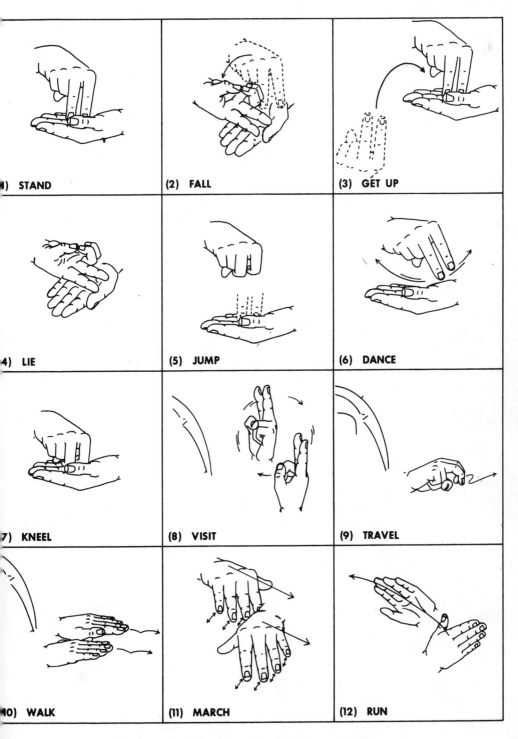

1) STAND	(2) FALL	(3) GET UP
4) LIE	(5) JUMP	(6) DANCE
7) KNEEL	(8) VISIT	(9) TRAVEL
10) WALK	(11) MARCH	(12) RUN

Note: Refer to description for explanation and synonyms.

SIT, CHAIR—The right curved index and middle fingers are placed crosswise on the left curved index and middle fingers, both palms facing down. (1)

> IDEA: Right hand represents someone sitting on the chair.

SIT DOWN (BE SEATED)—Both open hands point forward, palms down, are lowered slightly.

> IDEA: The natural motion of asking people to be seated.

ARISE—Both open hands pointing forward, palms up, are raised. (or, sign "STAND.")

> IDEA: The motion of asking people to rise.

CLIMB—Place the curved "V" hands before you facing each other; move them upward alternately in stages. (2)

REST—Fold the arms before the chest, one on top of the other. (3)

WORK—The right "S" facing down is struck several times on the wrist of the left "S." (4)

> IDEA: Activity of the hands.

FIGHT—Make the natural motion of fighting, using "S" hands. (5)

CONQUER, OVERCOME, DEFEAT, BEAT—Place the wrist of the right "S" against the side of the wrist of the left "S"; push the right "S" forward and down. (6)

> IDEA: Right hand represents the one who has conquered.

PLAY (Recreation)—Place the "Y" hands before you and shake them in and out from the wrists several times. (7)

> IDEA: Activity indicated by the hands.

PLAY (Musical instruments)—Imitate the motion of the instrument being played.

THROW—Throw the right "S" towards the left, opening the hand.

> IDEA: Natural motion of throwing.

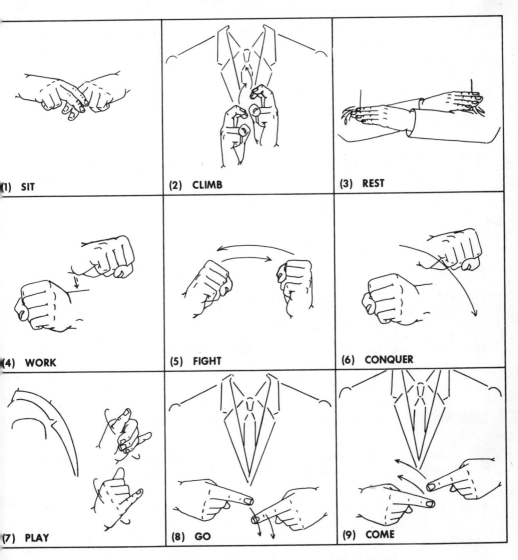

(1) SIT	(2) CLIMB	(3) REST
(4) WORK	(5) FIGHT	(6) CONQUER
(7) PLAY	(8) GO	(9) COME

Note: Refer to description for explanation and synonyms.

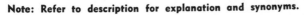

GO—Index fingers as they move forward, rotate around each other (palms toward self). (8)

> IDEA: Fingers going away from the body.

COME—Index fingers rotating around each other move toward the body, (palms toward self). (9)

> IDEA: Fingers coming toward the body.

TURN—Hold up the left index finger; point the right index finger down and circle it around the left index in a counterclockwise motion, the left index turning slightly. (1)

STRAY, DEVIATE (TO GO OFF THE TRACK)—Place both index fingers side by side (palms facing down) and then move the right index forward and away toward the right. (2)

HURRY—Move the right "H" forward with a quick up-and-down movement. (3)

ARRIVE, REACH—The right slightly bent hand moves forward and is placed into the left open palm. (4)

STAY—Place the thumb of the right "A" on the thumbnail of the left "A" and push downward slightly. (5)

CONTINUE—Place the thumb of the right "A" on the thumbnail of the left "A" and move both forward. (6)

FOLLOW—Place the right "A" behind the left "A" and move them both forward (7)

> IDEA: One hand follows the other.

CHASE—Sign "FOLLOW" more vigorously.

RACE, CONTEST—Place the "A" hands before you, palms facing each other, and move them back and forth alternately.

PASS—Move the right "A" forward past the left "A." (8)

LEAD—Grasp the tip of the left open hand with the right fingertips and thumb, and pull forward. (9)

> IDEA: Right hand leading the left.

ESCAPE, RUN AWAY—Place the right index under the left open hand which is facing down, and move it forward and out toward the right. (10)

DEPART, LEAVE—Place the open hands before you towards the right, palms down, with fingertips pointing forward; draw the hands back and up into "A" positions. (11)

LEAVE, NEGLECT—Place open hands before you, palm facing palm, tips pointing slightly to the right; give them a downward twist from the wrist. (12)

VERBS (continued)

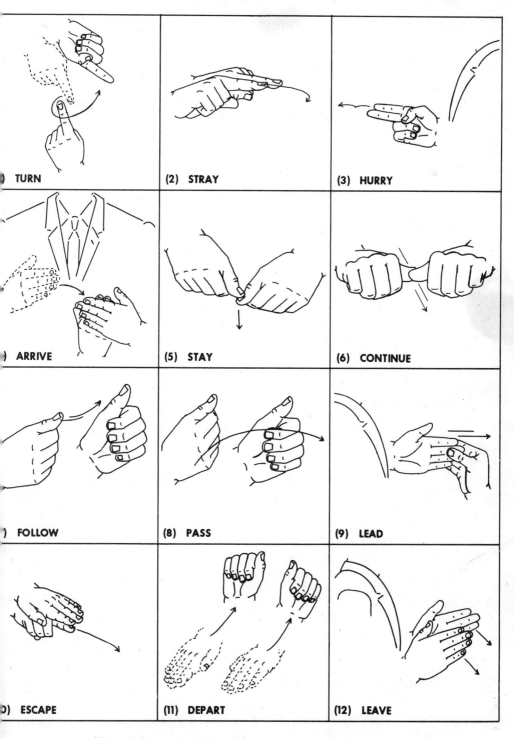

TURN   (2) STRAY   (3) HURRY

ARRIVE   (5) STAY   (6) CONTINUE

FOLLOW   (8) PASS   (9) LEAD

ESCAPE   (11) DEPART   (12) LEAVE

Note: Refer to description for explanation and synonyms.

LINE UP, QUEUE—Place the "FIVE" hands before you pointing up, right palm facing left and left palm facing right; the right thumbtip touches the tip of the little finger of the left hand. (1·)

> *IDEA: The fingers represent people standing in line.*

WAIT—Hold the left open hand, palm up, a little away from the left side; hold the right hand in the same position nearer the body, fingers pointing to the left wrist; wiggle the fingers of both hands. (2)

STOP—Little finger side of the right open hand is brought down sharply to a position across the left open palm. (3)

> *IDEA: The right hand is placed emphatically on the left to form a barrier.*

START, BEGIN—The tip of the right index makes a half-turn between the index and middle fingers of the left open hand. (4)

> *IDEA: Indicating a screw or a key being turned.*

DO, ACTIVITY—Place both "C" hands before you, palms down; move both hands to the right and left several times. (5)

MUST, NEED, NECESSARY, HAVE TO—The crooked index finger, pointing down moves downward forcefully. (6)

DEMAND, REQUEST, REQUIRE—Place the tip of the bent index finger in the left palm which is facing right, and draw both hands toward the body in this position. (The force used in making this sign determines which word is meant, i.e., "DEMAND" is made much more forcibly than "REQUEST.") (7)

COMPLETED, FINISHED—Hold the left "B" hand before you, palm toward self; move the little finger edge of the right open hand, palm facing left, along the forefinger edge of the left, dropping off at the edge. (8)

> *IDEA: Cut off at the end.*

FINISHED—This less formal sign for "FINISHED" is made by holding the "FIVE" hands before you palms toward the center and quickly turning them so the palms face down. (9)

BORN, BIRTH—Place the back of the right open hand on the left palm; bring the hands up and forward. (10)

LIVE—Both "A" hands, with thumbs pointing up, pass up the sides of the chest beginning at the waist. (11)

DIE, DEATH—Place right hand palm up and place left hand palm down in front of right; turn both hands over. (12)
(For "DYING," make the sign for "DIE" slowly.)

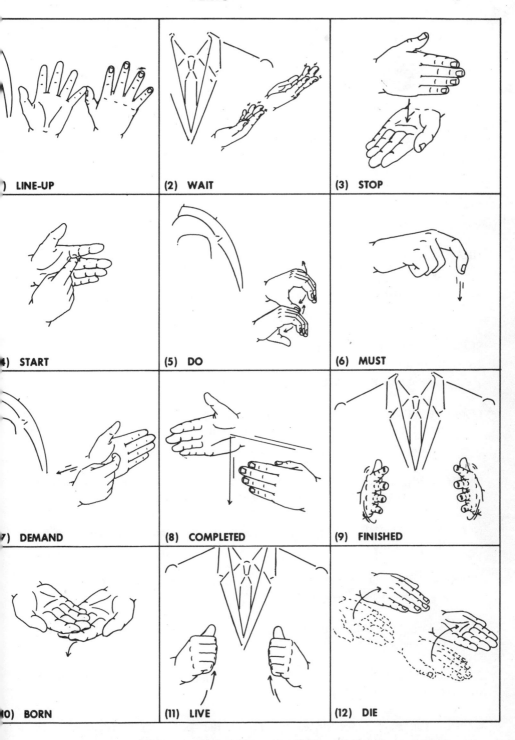

(1) LINE-UP	(2) WAIT	(3) STOP
(4) START	(5) DO	(6) MUST
(7) DEMAND	(8) COMPLETED	(9) FINISHED
(10) BORN	(11) LIVE	(12) DIE

Note: Refer to description for explanation and synonyms.

BREATHE, BREATH—Place both palms on the chest and move them in and out to indicate breathing. (1)

TASTE—Place the middle fingertip on the tip of the tongue, other fingers extended. (2)

> IDEA: *The finger placing something on the tongue to be tasted.*

SMELL—Place the palm before the nose and move it upward slightly several times. (3)

> IDEA: *Smelling something on the hand.*

TOUCH—Touch the back of the left hand with the right middle finger, other fingers extended. (4)

HEAR, EAR—The right index finger touches the ear.

LISTEN, HEARKEN—Place the "C" against the right ear.

> IDEA: *Cupping the hand over the ear in order to hear better.*

SEE—Place "V" before the face, fingertips near the eyes and move the hand forward. (5)

> IDEA: *Fingertips pointing to the eyes looking out.*

LOOK, WATCH—Place the "V" before the face, fingertips near the eyes, then turn the "V" so that the fingertips point forward. (6)

> IDEA: *"V" tips pointing to the place where the eyes are looking.*

SEARCH, SEEK, LOOK FOR, CURIOUS—The "C" hand with palm facing left, circles several times up-left-down-right before the face. (7)

NOTICE (OBSERVE)—Point to the eye with the right index finger and then touch the left palm. (8)

IMPRESS—Press the thumb of the right "A" hand into the left open palm and move the hands forward slightly. (9)

FLIRT—Place the thumbs of the "5" hands together, palms facing down; wiggle the fingers. (10)

CAN—With both hands in an "S" position, palms in, move them downward in a firm manner. (11)

CAN'T—The right index strikes the tip of the left index and passes it in a downward movement, both palms down. (12)

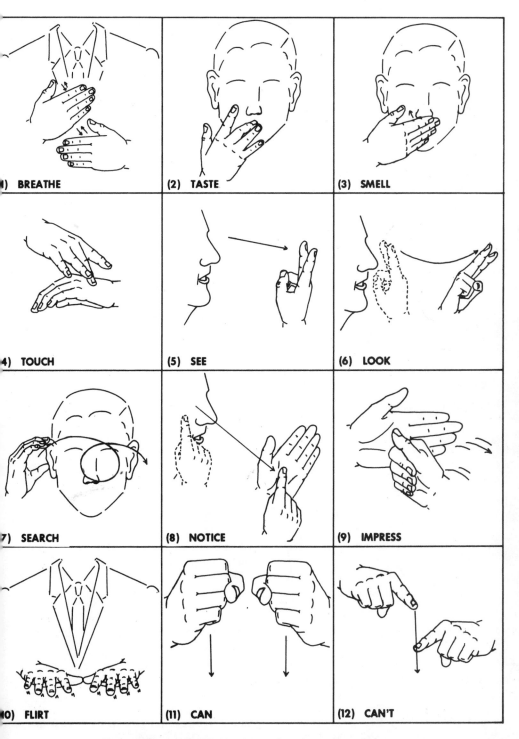

(1) BREATHE

(2) TASTE

(3) SMELL

(4) TOUCH

(5) SEE

(6) LOOK

(7) SEARCH

(8) NOTICE

(9) IMPRESS

(10) FLIRT

(11) CAN

(12) CAN'T

Note: Refer to description for explanation and synonyms.

MAY, MAYBE, PERHAPS—Both open hands, facing up and fingers pointing forward, are raised and lowered alternately. (1)

> IDEA: *The idea is being weighed.*

TRY—Place both "A" hands, facing each other, before you and push them forward with effort. (The sign is often made with the letter "T.")

> IDEA: *Pushing forward indicating effort.*

WILL—Raised right arm with open palm toward cheek, moves forward. (2)

> IDEA: *Moving ahead toward the future.*

WON'T, REFUSE—Hold up the right "S" hand, palm facing left and draw it back forcefully toward the right shoulder. (3)

> IDEA: *The closed fist draws back.*

DENY (to declare not to be true)—Place the thumb of the right "A" hand under the chin and push it forward; repeat with the left "A" and alternate several times.

DENY (self-denial)—With both hands in the "A" position, thumbs pointing down, push the hands down the chest a short distance. (4)

> IDEA: *The inner feelings which would rise are pushed down.*

HAVE, POSSESS—Place fingertips of both bent hands against the chest, palms facing self. (5)

> IDEA: *Holding the object against one's self.*

GIVE—Both "AND" hands facing down are turned in-up-forward, ending with palms open and facing up. (Sign can be reversed and brought towards self if this meaning is desired.) (6)

> IDEA: *Giving something to someone.*

GET, OBTAIN—Both open "5" hands palms facing each other close into "S" hands, the right on top of and touching the left. (7)

> IDEA: *Grasping something.*

RECEIVE—Sign "GET" and draw it towards self.

> IDEA: *Grasping something and taking it to one's self.*

WIN—Sign "GET" and "TRIUMPH."

ASSUME (i.e., taking up responsibility for a project, etc.)—Lift the open hands (palms facing down) and close them into "S" positions.

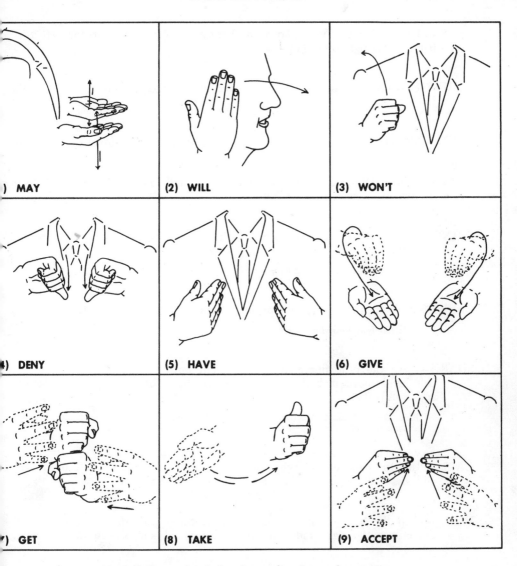

) MAY	(2) WILL	(3) WON'T
) DENY	(5) HAVE	(6) GIVE
) GET	(8) TAKE	(9) ACCEPT

Note: Refer to description for explanation and synonyms.

TAKE—Draw the open hand from right to left (palm facing left) ending in an "A" position. (8)

ACCEPT, WILLING—The open "AND" hands point toward each other, palms facing the body; move the hands toward the chest closing them into the "AND" position, the fingers touching the body. (9)

IDEA: Taking it to one's self.

KEEP—Place the right "V" hand palm leftward on the wrist of the left "V" hand, palm rightward. (1)

CAREFUL—Make the sign for "KEEP" and strike together several times at the wrist.

TAKE CARE OF—Make the sign for "KEEP" and circle it from right to left.

SERVE—With both palms facing up, move the hands alternately back and forth as if carrying a tray while walking. (2)

BRING—Bring both open hands toward self, palms facing up, one hand behind the other.
> IDEA: Carrying something and bringing it in.

CARRY—Both open hands, palms up, move from right to left before the body. (3)
> IDEA: Hands as if carrying something.

SHARE—Place the little finger side of the right open hand crosswise on the left palm and move it back and forth from the wrist (i.e., toward fingertips and back). (4)
> IDEA: As if dividing something that is in the hand and saying, "Some for you and some for me."

CALL—Place the palm of the right open hand on the back of the left open hand and draw the right up into an "A" position. (5)

WARN—Tap the back of the left hand several times with the right open hand. Sometimes the right index finger is also raised and shaken as if warning someone. (6)
> IDEA: As if tapping someone quickly to give warning.

SEND—Place the fingertips of the right bent hand on the back of the left open hand and lift the right hand straightening it into the open position, palm down. (7)

WELCOME—Bring the right open hand toward the body, palm facing up. (8)
> IDEA: Extending the hand in an invitation to come.

INVITE—Touch the back of the left hand with the palm of the right, and then make the sign for "WELCOME."

VERBS (continued)

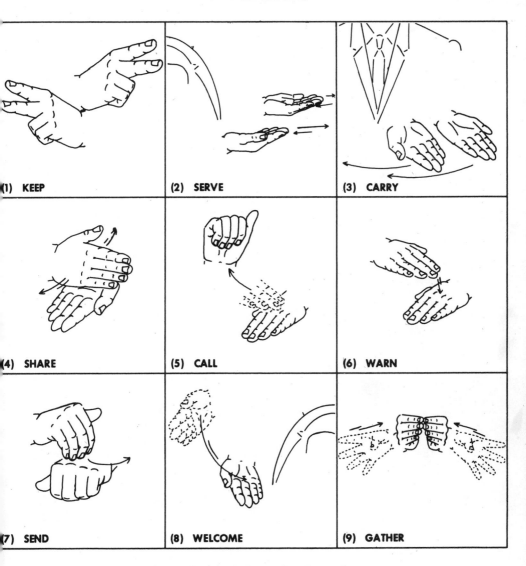

(1) KEEP

(2) SERVE

(3) CARRY

(4) SHARE

(5) CALL

(6) WARN

(7) SEND

(8) WELCOME

(9) GATHER

Note: Refer to description for explanation and synonyms.

GATHER, MEETING—Bring both open "AND" hands together from the sides into "AND" positions, so that the fingertips are touching and palms are facing each other. (9)

SCATTER—Place both "AND" hands together before you, palms down, and direct them forward and toward each side as the fingers open.

53

MEET—Bring both "G" hands together from the sides so that the palms meet. (1)

INTRODUCE—Hold both open hands before you somewhat apart with palms up; bring hands toward each other, tips pointing toward each other. (2)

CHOOSE, SELECT—With the thumb and forefinger of the right hand make a motion as if picking something first from the index and then from the middle finger of the left "V" hand which is facing you. (The sign is sometimes made with the right hand only.) (3)

    IDEA: Making a selection.

APPOINT—Extend the right hand and close the forefinger and thumb; draw the hand back and down in this position. (4)

SHOW, DEMONSTRATE—Place the tip of the right index into the left open hand which is facing out and move both hands forward. (5)

OFFER, TO PRESENT, PROPOSE—Place the open hands before you, palms up and fingers pointing forward; move the hands up and forward in this position. (6)

    IDEA: Indicates an object being held up and offered.

JOIN, CONNECT, BELONG—Hook the right index and thumb into the left index and thumb forming a chain (other three fingers are separated). (7)

BECOME—Place the slightly curved open hands before you, the right palm facing forward and the left facing it; turn hands so that they reverse positions. (8)

CHANGE—Using a modified "A" position in both hands place the right "A" so that the palm faces forward with the left "A" facing it; twist the hands around until they have reversed positions. (9)

INTERPRET—Make the sign for "CHANGE" using "F" hands. (10)

EXCHANGE, TRADE—Using the modified "A" position in both hands place the right "A" behind the left, draw it under and place it in front of the left while circling the left up and back so that the hands have changed relative positions. (11)

    IDEA: One hand changes place with the other.

POSTPONE, PROCRASTINATE, DELAY—Place both "F" hands before you, palms facing each other and fingers pointing forward; lift them up and forward and drop them; repeat several times moving ahead farther each time. (12)

    IDEA: The decision to act is moved farther and farther away.

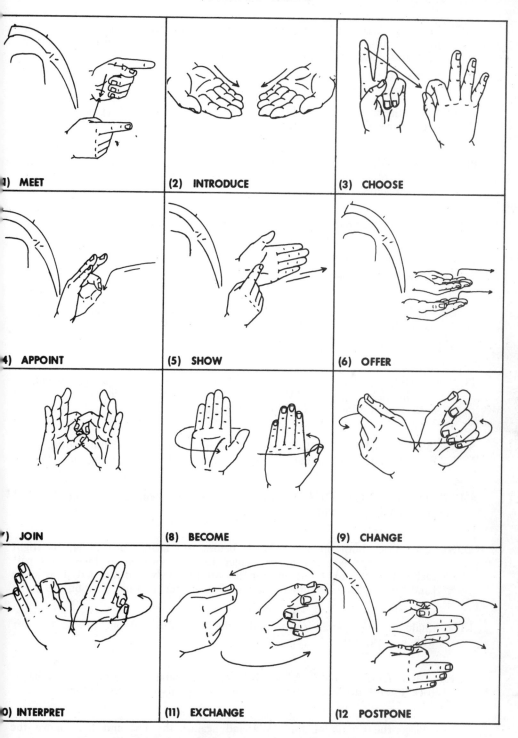

(1) MEET   (2) INTRODUCE   (3) CHOOSE

(4) APPOINT   (5) SHOW   (6) OFFER

(7) JOIN   (8) BECOME   (9) CHANGE

(10) INTERPRET   (11) EXCHANGE   (12 POSTPONE

Note: Refer to description for explanation and synonyms.

PUT, MOVE—Place the open "AND" hands before you, palms down, and lift them slightly, changing to the "AND" position as you move them to the right and down (fingertips pointing down all the while.) (1)

> IDEA: An object is lifted and placed.

MOVE (to stir into action)—Move the "AND" hands forward (pointing down), one behind the other, in a zigzag motion. (2)

PLAN, ARRANGE, PREPARE, READY, PUT IN ORDER—The open hands, facing each other, and pointing forward, are moved toward the right in several short sweeping motions. (3)

BOTHER, INTERFERE, PREVENT—Place the little finger edge of the right open hand between the thumb and forefinger of the left open hand and strike it several times. (4)

> IDEA: The right hand coming between.

VOLUNTEER—With the thumb and forefinger of the right hand grasp your lapel (or clothing if not wearing lapel) and pull it forward. (5)

> IDEA: Making it plain that one is available.

PUNISH—Hold the left "A" hand before you as if holding an imaginary culprit; use the right modified "A" as if holding a switch and move it back and forth several times as if administering punishment. (6)

SURRENDER, GIVE UP—Place both "A" hands before you, palms down; move them forward and up into a "5" position with palms facing out. (7)

DEFEND, PROTECT, GUARD—Place the left "S" behind the right "S" and push hands out slightly. (8)

DESTROY—Place both open "5" hands before you facing each other, the right lower than the left; the hands change to "A" positions as they brush past each other, the right one moving toward the body and the left away. The hands then pass each other again ending in the original position. (9)

KILL—Slide the right index finger under the left palm and out toward the left with a twist. (10)

BURY, GRAVE—Place both "A" hands before you, palms facing down; draw hands back toward the body into a curved hand position, palms still down. (11)

HIDE—Place the thumb of the "A" hand against the lips and then move the "A" hand under the left palm which is held before you. (12)

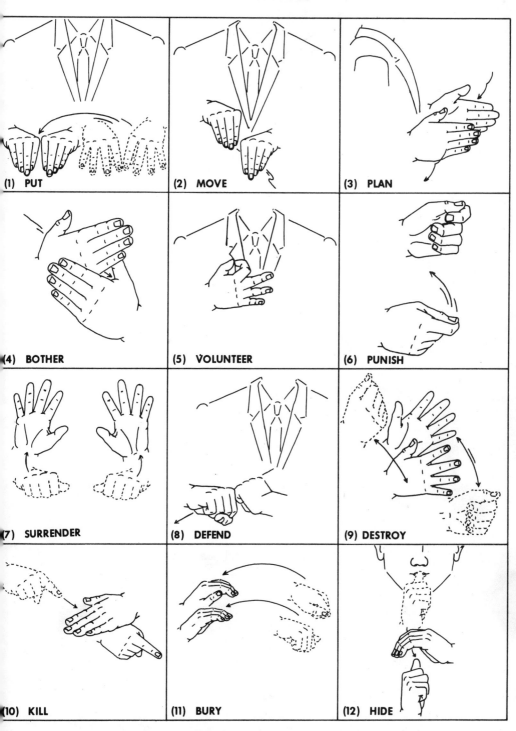

(1) PUT

(2) MOVE

(3) PLAN

(4) BOTHER

(5) VOLUNTEER

(6) PUNISH

(7) SURRENDER

(8) DEFEND

(9) DESTROY

(10) KILL

(11) BURY

(12) HIDE

Note: Refer to description for explanation and synonyms.

OPEN—Place both open hands side by side before the body; draw the hands apart toward the sides. (1)

CLOSE—Draw both open hands toward each other until the index fingers touch. (2)

MAKE—Place the right "S," palm facing left on the left "S," palm facing right; turn them so that palms face self and strike together again. Repeat several times. (3)

IDEA: As if twisting and pounding.

FIND—Place the open hand before you, palm down, draw the thumb and forefinger together and lift up as if picking up something. (4)

IDEA: The natural motion of picking up something.

LOSE—Both hands in the "AND" position, fingernails touching and palms facing up are dropped and opened. (5)

IDEA: The open hands dropping something.

HAPPEN—Point the index fingers up with palms facing self, then twist them forward so that the palms face forward. (6)

SUCCEED—Point both index fingers toward each other, palms facing self; turn and raise both hands so that the index fingers point up with palms facing out; repeat this motion several times, higher each time and end with index fingers pointing straight up. (7)

IDEA: Going higher and higher on a ladder.

HELP—Place the right open hand under the left "S" which is facing to the right; lift both hands together. (8)

IDEA: Right hand helping the left.

STEAL—Place the right "V" palm facing up, under the left elbow and bend it as it is drawn toward the wrist. (9)

TEMPT—Tap the left forearm near the elbow with the right index finger. (10)

IDEA: Tapping someone to entice them to do evil.

FAIL—Place the back of the right "V" in the left open palm and slide it forward and off. (11)

URGE—Using the modified "A" hands, place the right behind the left, and pull the hands toward the body in stages, as if pulling toward you with effort. (12)

IDEA: Trying to pull someone toward you.

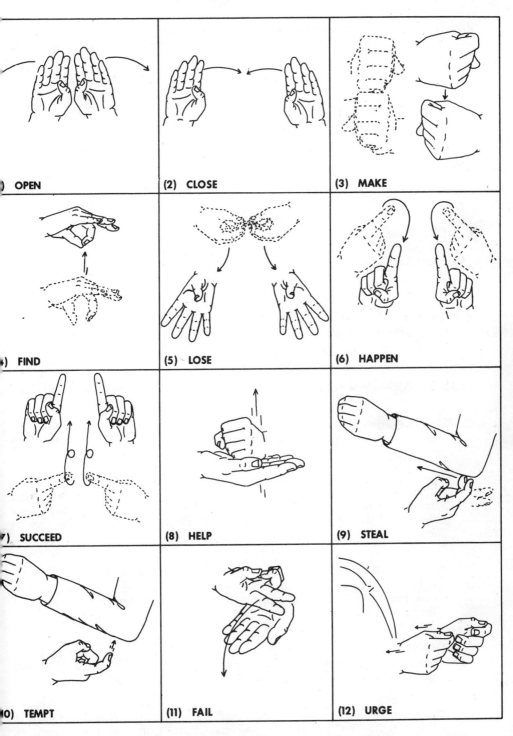

(1) OPEN

(2) CLOSE

(3) MAKE

(4) FIND

(5) LOSE

(6) HAPPEN

(7) SUCCEED

(8) HELP

(9) STEAL

(10) TEMPT

(11) FAIL

(12) URGE

Note: Refer to description for explanation and synonyms.

READ—Hold the left hand before you, palm up, fingers pointing to the right; point the right "V" to the top and move down as if scanning the page. (1)

IDEA: Left hand represents book and right "V" tips represent eyes scanning the page.

WRITE—Pressing the tip of the thumb and forefinger together, other fingers closed, write in the left palm. (2)

IDEA: Natural motion of writing.

COUNT—Close the right thumb and index fingertips (leaving other fingers extended) and move the tips up along the left palm which is facing right and pointing up. (3)

STUDY—Point the fingers of the right hand, palm down, at the left open hand; wiggle the fingers of the right hand as it is moved toward and away from the left hand. (4)

IDEA: Poring over a book.

GRADUATE—Describe a small clockwise circle with the right "G" hand and place it in the left palm. (5)

IDEA: Placing the seal on the diploma.

SEAL, STAMP—Strike the right "S" on the left palm, hold and then lift quickly. (6)

COPY—Place the tips of the right open "AND" hand against the palm of the left hand and then draw the right away into the closed "AND" position. (7)

IDEA: Taking something from an imaginary paper.

Another sign for "COPY" is frequently made when asking the deaf to "copy" a song or a prayer as in a church service. This is made by placing the left open hand before you, palm toward self and fingers pointing right; then place the tips of the open "AND" fingers against the back of the left and drawing away into a closed "AND" position.

IMPROVE—Place the left arm before you and strike the little finger side of the right open hand on the left wrist, move it up in stages striking the arm each time. (To indicate the opposite meaning, i.e., "deteriorate," move down the arm in stages.) (8)

CONDENSE—Bring the "C" hands toward the center and close them into "S" positions as the right little finger edge is placed on the forefinger thumb edge of the left fist.

EXPAND—Reverse the sign for "CONDENSE," i.e., place the little finger edge of the right "S" on the left "S" and draw them apart into a "C" position, right palm facing left and left palm facing right.

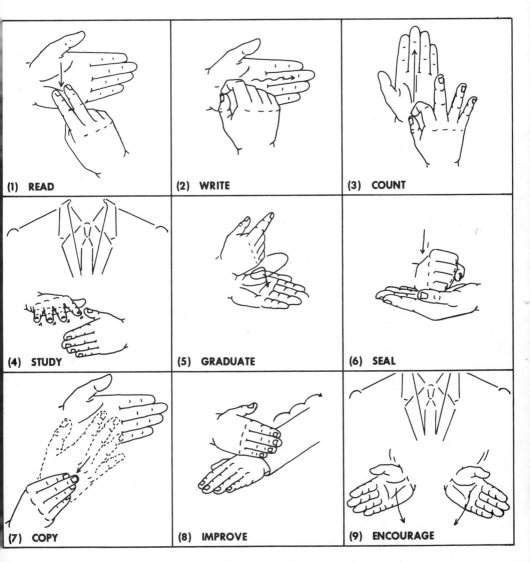

(1) READ (2) WRITE (3) COUNT

(4) STUDY (5) GRADUATE (6) SEAL

(7) COPY (8) IMPROVE (9) ENCOURAGE

Note: Refer to description for explanation and synonyms.

PUSH—Move the open hands forward, palms out, as if pushing an object.

ENCOURAGE—Move the open hands forward in stages with palms out as if
slightly pushing. (9)

IDEA: *Gently pushing in stages.*

MEASURE—Place the "Y" hands before·you, palms facing down and touch the thumb tips together several times. (1)

BUY—Place the back of the "AND" hand into the left palm and lift it out to the right, still in the "AND" position. (2)

> IDEA: *Putting out money.*

SELL—Both "AND" hands, pointing down, are held before you, moving back and forth from the wrist. (3)

> IDEA: *Holding up an item for sale.*

PAY—Place the tip of the right index finger in the left palm, and move the index finger out to the right. (4)

> IDEA: *Pointing to the money which is paid out.*

OWE, DEBT—The tip of the right index finger touches the center of the left palm several times. (5)

> IDEA: *Pointing to where the money belongs.*

EARN, GAIN—Draw the right curved hand across the left palm starting at the fingertips. (6)

SPEND, WASTE—Place the back of the right "AND" hand in the left palm and open it as you slide it off the fingertips. (7)

BORROW—Make the sign for "KEEP" and draw it toward the body.

LEND—Make the sign for "KEEP" and move it away from the body.

SAVE (AS, SAVING MONEY)—Place the inside of the right "V" against the back of the left wrist. (8)

SAFE, SAVE, RESCUE—Cross the "S" hands before you, both hands facing self as if bound at the wrists; turn both hands so that they are separated and facing forward. (9)

DELIVER—Make the sign for "SAVE" using either the "S" hands or the "D" hands.

FREE—Make the sign for "SAVE" using the "F" hands.

BOUND—Place the wrist of the right "S" (palm down) on the wrist of the left "S" (palm left) and push down slightly. (10)

BEG—Place the back of the right curved "5" hand on the back of the left hand; draw it back several times. (11)

COVER—Slide the right curved hand over the back of the left curved hand from right to left, both palms facing down. (12)

VERBS (continued)

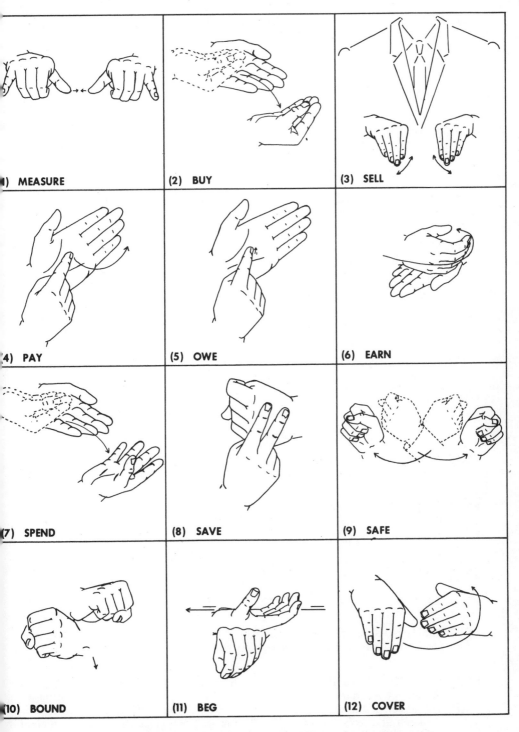

(1) MEASURE

(2) BUY

(3) SELL

(4) PAY

(5) OWE

(6) EARN

(7) SPEND

(8) SAVE

(9) SAFE

(10) BOUND

(11) BEG

(12) COVER

Note: Refer to description for explanation and synonyms.

BREAK—Hold the "S" hands side by side, palms down and give them a sudden outward twist as if holding an object in the hands and breaking it in two. (1)

VOTE—Touch the thumb and forefinger of the right hand (other fingers extended) and place in the left "O." (2)

COOPERATE—Place both curved "5" hands before you, palms facing self, and interlock the fingers beginning with the little finger (as gears fit together). Or, make the sign for "JOIN" and circle it from right to left before you. (3)

FORBID—Throw the side of the right "G" hand against the left palm which is pointing up and facing right. (4)

DEPEND—Place the right index and middle fingers on the back of the left index and middle fingers, both palms down, and push down slightly. (5)

> IDEA: One is leaning on the other.

USE—Circle the right "U" in a small clockwise motion. (The following sign for "WORN" and "USED" may also be used.)

WORN, USED—Place the right fingertips flat into the left palm and rub back and forth. (6)

FORCE—Place the right "C" (pointing forward) below the cheek and push forward. (7)

PERSECUTE, TEASE—Slide the right modified "A" across the top of the left modified "A" several times. (8)

EXCUSE, FORGIVE, PARDON—Wipe the little finger edge of the left palm with the tips of the right hand. (9)

> IDEA: Wiping off the guilt.

SUPPORT—Place the right "S" under the left "S" and push upward. (10)

> IDEA: The right hand supports the left.

ESTABLISH, FOUNDED—Using the right "A," make a clockwise circle and then place the little finger edge firmly on the back of the left closed fist. (11)

BLAME, FAULT—Place the right "A" with thumb pointing up, on the back of the left closed hand. (When this sign is made and the right "A" is raised and directed outward, it means "your fault"; when raised and directed toward self it means "my fault.") "Innocence" is signed by a combination of "BLAME" and "NOT." (12)

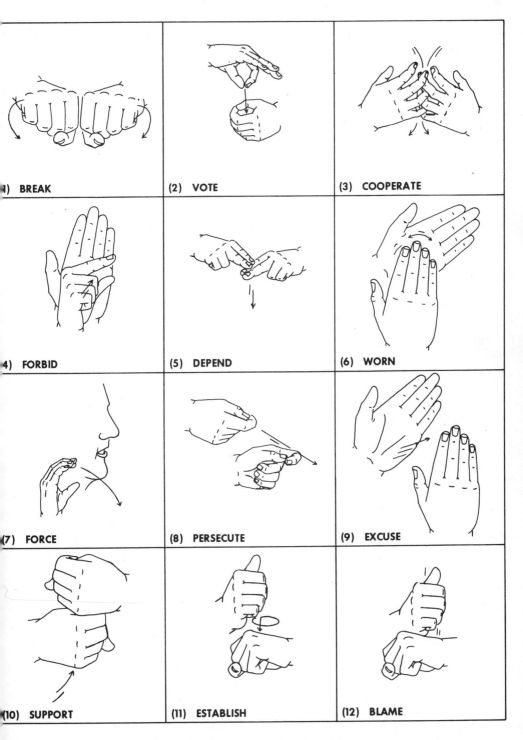

(1) BREAK

(2) VOTE

(3) COOPERATE

(4) FORBID

(5) DEPEND

(6) WORN

(7) FORCE

(8) PERSECUTE

(9) EXCUSE

(10) SUPPORT

(11) ESTABLISH

(12) BLAME

Note: Refer to description for explanation and synonyms.

REIGN, RULE, CONTROL, IN CHARGE OF, AUTHORITY—Using both modified "A" hands, move them back and forth as if holding reins. (1)

ALLOW, LET, PERMIT—Both open hands with fingers pointing forward, palms facing in, are bent upward from the wrist till the fingers point slightly upward and outward (the heels of the hands being closer together than the tips of the fingers). (2)

EAT—The "AND" hand is thrown lightly toward the mouth several times. (3)
> IDEA: Food is put to the mouth.

FEED—Place the tips of the right "AND" hand at the mouth; then move both "AND" hands away from the mouth, palms up, one behind the other. (4)

DRINK—Place the "C" hand before the mouth, palm facing left, and make a motion as if pouring a drink into the mouth. (5)
> IDEA: Natural motion of drinking.

DRINK (liquor)—Place the thumb of the "Y" hand at the mouth.

SMOKING—Place the right "V" at the lips.

SLEEP—Draw the open fingers down over the face into an "AND" position near the chin, bowing the head slightly. (6)

AWAKEN—Place both "Q" hands at the sides of the eyes, forefinger and thumb touching, then separate the thumb and index. (7)
> IDEA: Eyes opening.

WASH—Rub the "A" hands together, palm to palm.
> IDEA: Natural motion of washing by hand.

IRON—Slide the right "A" hand back and forth, palm down, across the left palm.
> IDEA: Natural motion of ironing.

BATHE—Rub the "A" hands on the chest near the shoulder. (8)
> IDEA: As if washing the body.

COOK—Place the back of the right open hand into the left palm and turn the right over ending palm to palm.
> IDEA: Pancake being turned over.

SEW—With the right "F" holding an imaginary needle and the left "O" holding the cloth, go through the motion of sewing.
> IDEA: Natural motion of sewing.

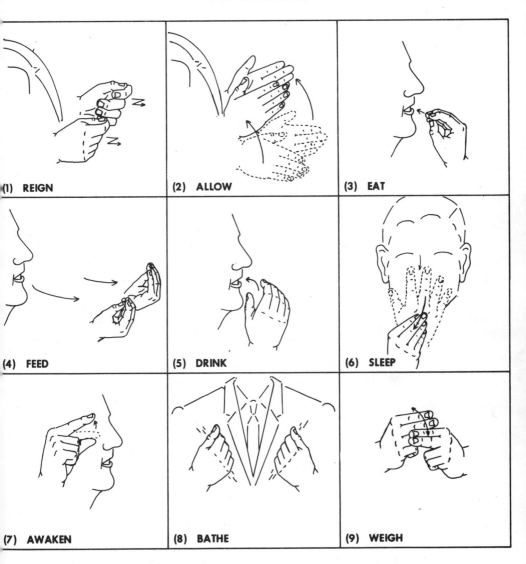

(1) REIGN   (2) ALLOW   (3) EAT

(4) FEED   (5) DRINK   (6) SLEEP

(7) AWAKEN   (8) BATHE   (9) WEIGH

Note: Refer to description for explanation and synonyms.

CUT, SCISSOR—Using the index and middle fingers of the right hand, imitate the cutting motion of a scissor. Or, draw the thumbnail of the right "A" across the left palm indicating an imaginary gash.

WEIGH—Place the middle finger of the right "H" across the index finger of the left "H" and balance the right "H" on the left, similar to the motion of a seesaw. (9)

SHAVE—Draw the outside edge of the thumb of the right "Y" hand down the cheek as if shaving. (1)

FISHING—Place the right modified "A" hand behind the left modified "A" hand and make a quick upward turn from both wrists. (2)

HUNT, SHOOT, GUN—Point the right "L" forward, palm facing left, and move the thumb up and down.

DROWN, SINK—Place the right "V," palm toward self, between the index and middle fingers of the left open hand which is facing down, and slide it down with a slight wavy motion. (3)

PRINT—The right "G" palm down, picks the imaginary type and places it in the left palm. (4)

> IDEA: Natural motion of old-style typesetting.

DRAW (ART)—Using the right "I" as an imaginary brush, draw a wavy line down the left palm. (5)

PAINT—Using the fingertips of the right open hand as a brush, draw them back and forth across the left palm.

PRACTICE—Rub the "A" hand back and forth along the outside edge of the left index finger. (6)

BUILD—Place the palm of one hand on the back of the other; alternate hands and repeat several times. (7)

PLANT—With the fingers pointing down, pass the thumb across the inside of the fingertips from the little finger to the forefinger and move the hand across from left to right as if planting seed. (8)

REAP, HARVEST—1) Use the left hand to hold imaginary stalks and use the right modified "A" to imitate the motion of cutting the stalks. Or, 2) Use the right open hand and sweep across the left palm into an "A" position as if gathering in the harvest. (9)

VERBS (continued)

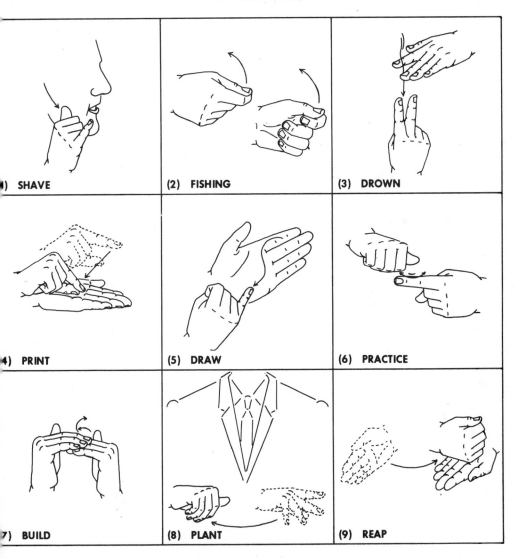

(1) SHAVE

(2) FISHING

(3) DROWN

(4) PRINT

(5) DRAW

(6) PRACTICE

(7) BUILD

(8) PLANT

(9) REAP

Note: Refer to description for explanation and synonyms.

CHAPTER IX

COMMUNICATION

SIGNS, THE LANGUAGE OF: DACTYLOLOGY—Cross the index fingers before you, palms facing out, and circle the arms alternately toward the body. (1)

> IDEA: Hands are moved representing signs.

LANGUAGE, SENTENCE—The thumb and index fingertips of both hands (with other fingers extended) are pulled apart in a twisting motion. (2)

FINGER SPELLING, MANUAL ALPHABET—The right "5" hand with palm down moves from left to right, fingers wiggling. (3)

> IDEA: Indicating the movement of fingers spelling.

SPEECH READING, LIP READING—Describe a circle around the lips with the bent "V," palm facing in. (4)

> IDEA: The sign for "READ" is directed to the lips.

HARD-OF-HEARING—Make an "H" and describe a small arc to the right.

DEAF—Touch the right ear and then sign "CLOSED." (The sign for "DEAF" is commonly made by touching the ear and then the mouth with the tip of the index finger.)

HEARING (referring to a hearing person)—Sign "SPEAK."

> IDEA: Indicates that hearing people have the ability to speak.

VOICE—Place the tips of the "V" at the throat and draw them up towards the chin.

SPEAK, SAY, TELL—The index finger, pointing to the left, is held before the mouth and rolls forward in a circular movement. (5)

> IDEA: Words proceeding from the mouth.

ANNOUNCE, PROCLAIM—Index fingers touch the lips and are drawn forward and out, away from the face. (6)

> IDEA: The sign for "TELL" is enlarged.

ASK—Place open hands palm to palm and draw them toward the body.

> IDEA: Hands held as in prayer.

ANSWER, REPLY—Place the tip of the right index, palm facing left, at the lips; place the left index, pointing up, in front of it; move both hands out ending with the index fingers pointing forward. (7)

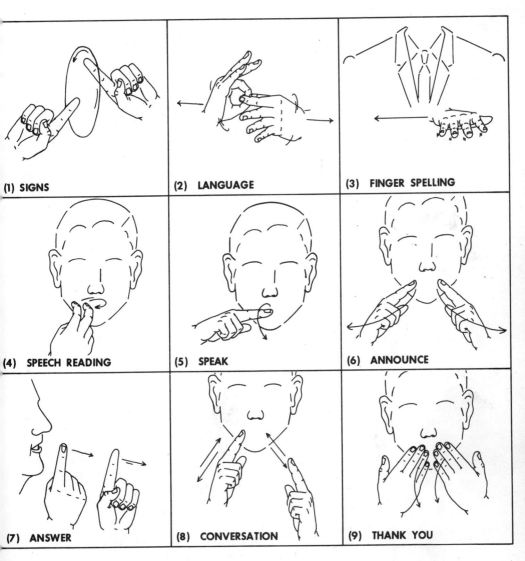

(1) SIGNS (2) LANGUAGE (3) FINGER SPELLING

(4) SPEECH READING (5) SPEAK (6) ANNOUNCE

(7) ANSWER (8) CONVERSATION (9) THANK YOU

Note: Refer to description for explanation and synonyms.

CONVERSATION, TALK—Place the tips of the index fingers on the lips and move them forward and back alternately. (8)

> IDEA: Talking back and forth.

THANK YOU, YOU'RE WELCOME, HELLO, GOODBYE—Place the tips of the open hands against the mouth and throw them forward (similar to throwing a kiss). (9)

EXPLAIN, DESCRIBE—Place the "F" hands before you, palms facing each other and fingers pointing forward; move the hands forward and back alternately. (1)

STORY, MESSAGE—The thumb and index fingertips of both hands (with other fingers extended) are pulled apart several times. (2)

GOSSIP—The thumb and index fingertips of both hands (with other fingers closed) face each other and open and close. (3)

> IDEA: Two mouths opening and closing.

COMMAND—Sign "SPEAK" large and with force.

CRITICIZE, CANCEL—Draw an "X" into the left palm with the right index finger.

WHISPER—Place the right curved hand at the right side of the mouth, palm facing left.

> IDEA: Hiding the mouth while talking.

LECTURE, SPEECH, TESTIMONY—Hold the right open hand to the side with palm facing left and fingers pointing up; move the hand from the wrist forward and back several times. (4)

> IDEA: A gesture made in public speaking.

PROMISE—Place the index finger at the mouth and then place the right open palm on the index-finger side of the left "S" hand. (5)

VOW, SWEAR, TAKE OATH, LOYAL—Place the index finger at the mouth and then raise the right hand, palm facing forward while the fingertips of the left hand, palm facing down, touch the right elbow. (6)

> IDEA: Raising the right hand as if taking an oath.

QUESTION—Draw a question mark in the air with the index finger.

YES—Hold the "S" hand before you, palm facing out, and bend the wrist forward. This sign may be made with the "Y" hand shaken several times to indicate agreement.

NO—Make an abbreviated "N" and "O" by bringing the index, middle finger, and thumb together in one motion.

SCOLD—Shake the index finger in a natural motion of scolding.

MOCK, SCORN, RIDICULE—Draw the right index finger back from the mouth and direct both hands forward (right behind left) with the index and little fingers extended. (7)

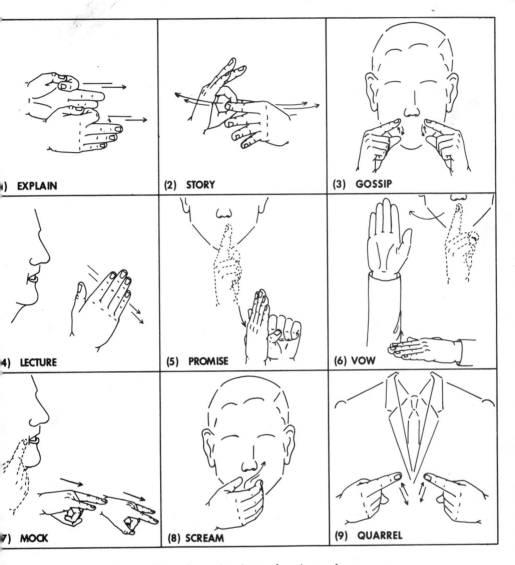

(1) EXPLAIN | (2) STORY | (3) GOSSIP

(4) LECTURE | (5) PROMISE | (6) VOW

(7) MOCK | (8) SCREAM | (9) QUARREL

Note: Refer to description for explanation and synonyms.

SCREAM, SHOUT, CRY OUT—Place the right "C" hand at the mouth, palm facing self and move it upward in a wavy motion. (8)

QUARREL—Point both index fingers toward each other, palms facing self, and shake the hands up and down from the wrist simultaneously. (9)

IDEA: Imitation of roosters fighting.

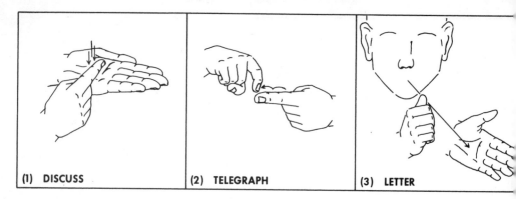

| (1) DISCUSS | (2) TELEGRAPH | (3) LETTER |

Note: Refer to description for explanation and synonyms.

DISCUSS—Strike the side of the index finger into the left palm several times. (1)

DEBATE, ARGUE—Make the sign for "DISCUSS" alternately with the right and left hands.

TELEGRAPH—Using the right "X" make a series of dots along the edge of the left index finger. (2)

TELEPHONE—Hold the right "S" to the ear and the left "S" to the mouth as if using a telephone.

RADIO—Hold the cupped hands over the ears.
> IDEA: The old-fashioned headsets used with the radio.

TV—Spell the letters "TV."

LETTER—Place the thumb of the right "A" hand against the mouth and then into the left palm. (3)
> IDEA: Stamping a letter.

CHAPTER X

NATURE

EARTH—Place the thumb and middle finger of the right hand on the back of the left hand near the wrist and rock the right back and forth. (1)

> IDEA: *The earth rotating on its axis.*

WORLD—Circle the right "W" forward-down-up around the left "W" and place it on the side of the left hand. (2)

> IDEA: *The world going around.*

LAND, FIELD—Rub the fingertips of both hands with the thumb as if feeling soil; make a counterclockwise circle with the right open hand, palm down. (3)

> IDEA: *Feeling the soil and indicating a large area.*

SKY, HEAVENS—Make a sweeping motion with the open hand left to right, above eye level.

> IDEA: *Indicating the expanse of the skies.*

SUN—Draw a clockwise circle in the air.

> IDEA: *Indicate the sun by a round circle overhead.*

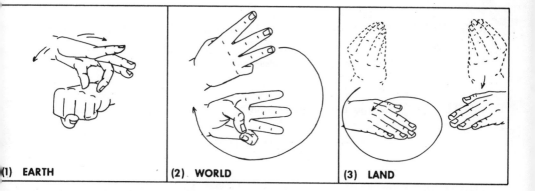

| (1) EARTH | (2) WORLD | (3) LAND |

SUNSHINE—Sign "SUN"; then place both "AND" hands high, right behind the left and open the fingers as the hands are moved forward, palms facing down and fingers pointing forward. (1)

> IDEA: The rays of the sun coming down.

MOON—Place the "C" hand over the right eye, palm facing left. (2)

STAR—Using both index positions, palms facing forward and fingers pointing up, move the right index up along the side of the left index, alternating hands, and repeat several times. (3)

WATER—Strike the side of the mouth several times with the index finger of the "W" hand. (4)

RAIN—Sign "WATER"; then lower both "5" hands with palms down and fingers wiggling. (5)

> IDEA: Water coming down.

SNOW—Sign "WHITE"; then lower both "5" hands with palms down and fingers wiggling.

> IDEA: Something white coming down.

FLOOD—Place both "5" hands before you, palms down and fingers pointing forward; wiggle the fingers as hands are raised.

> IDEA: The water level is rising.

ICE, FREEZE—Place both "5" hands before you, palms down, and drop them slightly coming to a sudden stop as the fingers bend. (6)

> IDEA: The water coming down suddenly freezes.

LIGHTNING—Use the index finger pointing up and make a quick zigzag motion in the air. (7)

> IDEA: The quick movement of lightning in the skies.

THUNDER—Point to the ear, then place the "S" hands before you, palms down bringing the right hand toward self and the left toward the side; reverse and repeat several times. (8)

> IDEA: Movement of the fists represents vibrations.

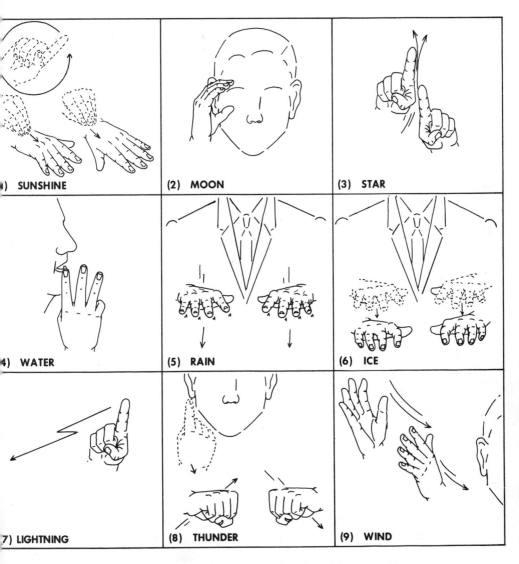

(1) SUNSHINE	(2) MOON	(3) STAR
(4) WATER	(5) RAIN	(6) ICE
(7) LIGHTNING	(8) THUNDER	(9) WIND

Note: Refer to description for explanation and synonyms.

EARTHQUAKE—Sign "EARTH" and finish with the "S" hands as in "THUNDER."

WIND—Hold the hands high, palms toward each other, the left slightly lower than the right; move them towards the left in several short sweeping motions. (9)

IDEA: *Sweeping movement of the wind.*

CLOUD—Place the slightly curved "5" hand, palm down, above the left upturned slightly curved "5" hand; swirl the hands around toward the left. (1)

SHADOW—Sign "BLACK"; then make a counterclockwise circle with the right open hand, palm down, over the upturned left hand. (2)

ROCK, STONE—Strike the back of the left "S" hand with the palm side of the right "A"; then place the "C" hands before you, facing each other, forming the shape of a rock.

MOUNTAIN—Strike the back of the left "S" hand with the palm side of the right "A"; then raise both open hands toward the side, one behind the other as if indicating the side of a mountain. (3)

VALLEY—Place both open hands high on each side, palms down and bring them down and then together (index sides touching) indicating the sides of mountains with the valley in the center. (4)

TREE—Hold the right arm up before you, placing the elbow into the left palm; shake the right "5" hand in and out rapidly several times. (5)

RIVER—Sign "WATER" ("W" at the side of the mouth); then place the left hand behind the right, palms down and wiggle the fingers as the hands are moved toward the right. (6)

    IDEA: Water that flows.

OCEAN, SEA—Sign "WATER"; then place the left hand behind the right, palms down and move the hands up and down to indicate the waves of the ocean. (7)

    IDEA: Water and waves.

SHORE—Place the back of the right hand against the palm of the left (right hand pointing left and left hand pointing right). Repeat several times, moving in this position from right to left.

    IDEA: One hand represents the water and the other the land. Indicating the water touching the shore.

SPRING, FOUNTAIN—Push up the right "AND" hand (with palm facing left and fingers pointing up) through the left "C," opening it and wiggling the fingers as it is moved up, over and down to indicate water flowing over the edge.

GRASS—Sign "GREEN" and "GROW."

FLOWER—Place the tips of the "AND" hand first under one nostril then under the other. (8)

    IDEA: Smelling the flowers.

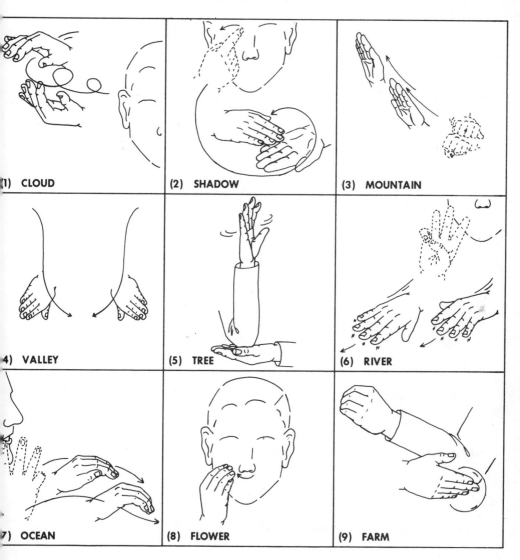

(1) CLOUD

(2) SHADOW

(3) MOUNTAIN

(4) VALLEY

(5) TREE

(6) RIVER

(7) OCEAN

(8) FLOWER

(9) FARM

Note: Refer to description for explanation and synonyms.

GARDEN—Using both "A" hands as if holding a hoe, go through the motion of hoeing. Or, indicate a fence by using the "4" hands and then sign "FLOWERS."

FARM—Rub the under side of the left arm near the elbow with the right open hand. Or, move the little-finger edge of the right hand (slightly slanted) across the left palm indicating the action of a plow. (9)

CHAPTER XI

QUANTITY, SIZE, AND DEGREE

MANY—Hold both "S" hands before you, palms facing up and open them quickly several times. (1)

> IDEA: All the fingers opening up indicate a great number.

FEW, SEVERAL—The right "A" hand, with palm facing up, opens slowly as the thumb passes along the inside of the opening fingers. (2)

> IDEA: A small number is indicated by the fingers opening one by one.

BOTH—Pass the right "2" hand down through the right "C," left hand ending with the two fingers together (both palms facing self). (3)

SOME, PART—Place the little-finger side of the right curved hand into the left palm; draw the right hand toward self and straighten it. (4)

> IDEA: Indicating a part of what is in the hand.

NONE, NO—Place the "O" hands before you, palms facing out; bring both hands to the sides, still in the "O" position.

NOTHING—Place the "O" hands before you, palms facing out; bring both hands to the sides opening into the "5" position, palms forward. (5)

> IDEA: Hands open completely to indicate there is nothing in them.

MORE—Bring the tips of both "AND" hands together. (6)

MOST—Sign "MORE" and then lift the right "A" hand, with thumb pointing up.

-ER (Comparative degree)—When "ER" is added to a word to form the comparative degree, make the following sign:
Raise the right "A" up and past the left "A," both thumbs pointing up. (7)

-EST (Superlative degree)—When "EST" is added to a word to form the superlative degree, make the sign for "ER" but raise the right "A" several inches higher.

AND—Place the right hand before you, fingers spread apart and pointing left (palm facing self), draw the hand to the right, closing the tips. (8)

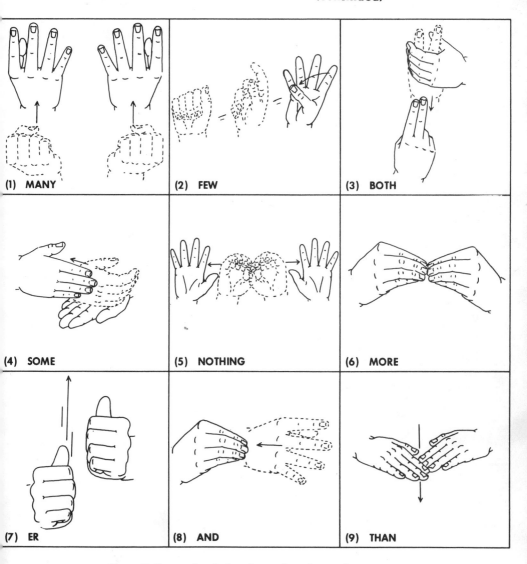

(1) MANY	(2) FEW	(3) BOTH
(4) SOME	(5) NOTHING	(6) MORE
(7) ER	(8) AND	(9) THAN

Note: Refer to description for explanation and synonyms.

TOO, ALSO—Make the sign for "SAME" twice—once before you and again to the left.

AS—Place the index fingers side by side several inches apart, palms down, and move them over to the left in this position.

THAN—Place the left open hand before you, palm down and brush the index-finger edge of the right open hand off the fingertips of the left and down. (9)

QUANTITY, SIZE, AND DEGREE (continued)

ABOUT—Place the left "AND" hand before you pointing right and use the right index to circle around the tips up-forward-down-in. (1)

EXCEPT—Grasp the end of the left index finger (which is pointing up) with the tips of the right and pull up. (2)

LARGE, GREAT—Tips of the "L" hands touch and are drawn apart. (3)

VERY—Place the tips of the "V" hands together and pull them apart. (4)

MUCH—Hold both hands before you, palm facing palm, with fingers slightly spread and curved; draw hands apart. (5)

SMALL—Hold both slightly curved hands before you, palm facing palm, and push hands toward each other several times.

LITTLE—Using an "X" position, rub the end of the thumb against the end of the index finger, palm facing up. (6)

> IDEA: Just as little as might be on a fingertip.

HALF—Hold out the left index finger, pointing toward the right, palm in; place the right index across it and draw it back toward self. Or, place the little-finger edge of the right open hand across the left palm and draw it back toward self.

WIDE—Place both open hands before you, palm facing palm, and draw them apart. (7)

NARROW—Place both open hands before you some distance apart, palm facing palm, and bring them toward each other.

WIDTH—Place both open hands before you some distance apart, palm facing palm; move them toward each other and out again several times.

HEAVY—Place both open hands before you, palms facing up and drop them slightly as if holding too heavy an object.

LIGHT (in weight)—Place both open hands before you, palms facing up, and raise hands slightly as if lifting a light object.

LIMIT—Place the right bent hand several inches above the left bent hand; bring both hands forward a short distance. (8)

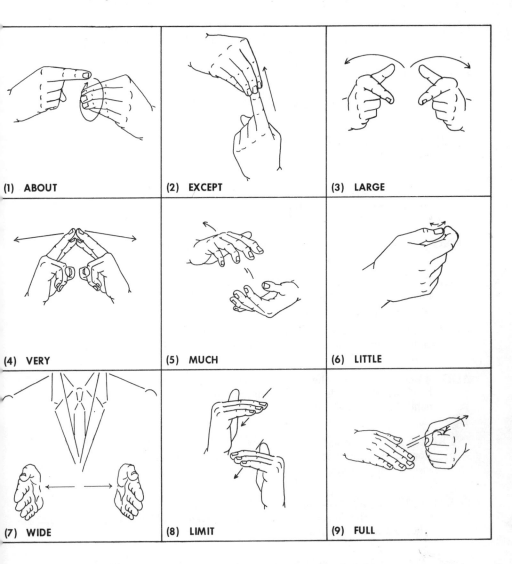

(1) ABOUT	(2) EXCEPT	(3) LARGE
(4) VERY	(5) MUCH	(6) LITTLE
(7) WIDE	(8) LIMIT	(9) FULL

Note: Refer to description for explanation and synonyms.

FULL—Place the right open hand on the left "S" (palm facing right) and brush across it to the left. (9)

> IDEA: Filled to the brim.

ENOUGH, PLENTY—Place the right open hand on the left "S" (palm facing right) and brush across it to the right several times.

ALMOST, NEARLY—With both open palms facing up, place the little-finger edge of the right under the fingertips of the left and draw up. (1)

EXCEED, EXCESSIVE—Place the fingers of the right bent hand on the backs of the fingers of the left bent hand (right tips pointing left and left tips pointing right); raise the right hand in this position several inches. (2)

TALL—Pass the right index finger up along the left palm which is pointing upward. (3)

SHORT (stature)—Hold the right open hand before you, palm facing down, raising and lowering it several times.

LONG—Draw the right index finger up along the left arm. (4)

SHORT (in length)—Rub the middle finger of the right "H" hand back and forth along the index finger of the left "H." (5)

DECREASE—Hold the open hands before you some distance apart, right above left, palms facing each other and bring them toward each other in stages. (6)

ADD—Place the tips of the right "AND" hand on the tips of the left "AND" hand which has the palm facing up; repeat several times bringing the left hand higher each time.

INCREASE—Hold the left "H" before you, palm facing down; bring the right "H" from a palm-up position to a palm-down position on the left "H"; repeat several times. Or, make the sign for "ADD" several times. (7)

SUBTRACT, REMOVE—Hold the left open hand before you palm facing rightward; place the fingertips of the right curved hand (palm down) against the left palm and move it down ending in an "A" position. (8)

MULTIPLY—Place both "V" hands before you, palms facing self, and cross them so that the back of the right "V" passes against the palm of the left "V." (9)

ARITHMETIC—Use the sign for "MULTIPLY" repeating the motion several times. (This sign is used for all calculation.)

DIVIDE—Using the index fingers, trace in the air the signs used in long division. Or, place the little-finger edge of the right open hand crosswise on the index-finger edge of the left open hand; .draw both hands to the sides ending with palms down.

PER CENT—Using the "O" hand, draw a per cent sign in the air.

QUANTITY, SIZE, AND DEGREE (continued)

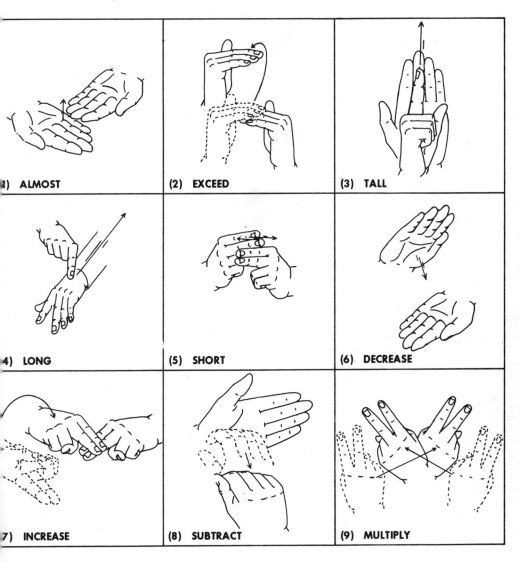

(1) ALMOST	(2) EXCEED	(3) TALL
(4) LONG	(5) SHORT	(6) DECREASE
(7) INCREASE	(8) SUBTRACT	(9) MULTIPLY

Note: Refer to description for explanation and synonyms.

CHAPTER XII

QUALITY, KIND, AND CONDITION

GOOD—Touch the lips with the fingers of the right hand and then move the right hand forward placing it palm up into the palm of the left hand. (1)

> IDEA: It has been tasted and smelled and offered as acceptable.

BETTER—Place the open hand before the mouth, palm facing in and fingers pointing left; then draw it up into an "A" position. (2)

BEST—The same sign is used as for "BETTER" except that the "A" is raised higher.

BAD—Touch the lips with the fingers of the right hand and then turn the palm down. (3)

> IDEA: It has been tasted and smelled and turned down.

POOR—The open fingers of the right hand are placed at the left elbow and pulled downward several times. (4)

> IDEA: Indicating the ragged sleeve

RICH—Place the back of the right "AND" hand in the left Palm and then lift it out, opening the fingers, palm still facing up. (5)

> IDEA: Money falling through the fingers into the left hand.

EXPENSIVE—Place the back of the right "AND" hand into the left palm; lift the right hand out and draw it away, opening it somewhat and then giving it a slight quick twist to the right.

CHEAP, INEXPENSIVE—Sign "MONEY" and then direct the open palms toward each other several times to indicate "SMALL."

EASY—Place the curved left hand before you palm facing up. Using the little-finger side of the open right hand, brush under the fingertips of the left hand and upward several times. (6)

> IDEA: The fingertips of the left easily yield to the right.

HARD—Strike the middle finger of the right bent "V" on the back of the left "S." Or, strike the back of the right "S" on the back of the left "S." (7)

> IDEA: Back of the hand is hard.

FAST, QUICK, IMMEDIATELY—The right thumb is snapped out of the curved index finger as if shooting a marble. (8)

> IDEA: As fast as shooting a marble.

SLOW—Stroke down the back of the left hand slowly with the right hand.

> IDEA: The hand is moving slowly.

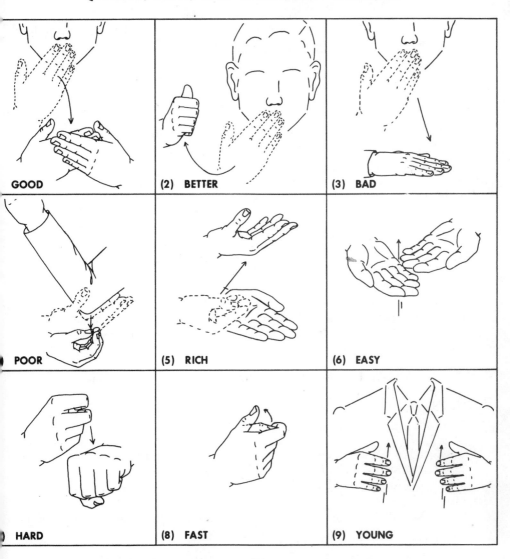

GOOD	(2) BETTER	(3) BAD
POOR	(5) RICH	(6) EASY
HARD	(8) FAST	(9) YOUNG

Note: Refer to description for explanation and synonyms.

YOUNG—Place the fingertips of both open hands on the chest, several inches apart, and brush upwards several times. (9)

OLD—The right "C" hand grasps an imaginary beard at the chin and moves downward into an "S" position.

    IDEA: Age is signified by a beard.

NEW, NEWS—The left open hand faces up; the back of the right open hand brushes across the heel of the left from right to left. (1)

HONEST, TRUTH—Place the middle finger of the right "H" on the left palm near the wrist and move it forward toward the fingertips. (2)

> IDEA: *Divided in half honestly.*

TRUE, TRULY, VERILY—Touch tip of right index finger to the mouth, palm facing left and move it slightly up and forward. (3)

> IDEA: *Speaking straight.*

FALSE—The right index finger pointing up with palm facing left, is brushed across the lips from right to left. (4)

> IDEA: *The truth is brushed aside.*

LIE, UNTRUTH—Right index finger, palm facing down, passes across the lips from right to left. (5)

> IDEA: *Not straight forward as in "TRUTH" but to the side.*

RIGHT, CORRECT—The little-finger edge of the right "G" hand is placed on the index of the left "G" hand so that both index fingers point forward, one above the other. (6)

WRONG, MISTAKE—The "Y" hand touches the chin, palm facing in. (7)

STRONG, POWERFUL, MIGHTY—Bring the "S" hands down with force. (8)

> IDEA: *The fists represent power.*

WEAK—Place the four fingertips of the right hand in the left palm; then bend the fingers of the right hand.

> IDEA: *Weak in the knees.*

TIRED, WEARY—Fingertips of the bent hands are placed at each side of the waist and then droop slightly. (9)

SICK—Touch forehead with right fingertips and stomach with left fingertips. (Sometimes only the tip of the middle finger is used.) (10)

> IDEA: *Head and stomach are affected.*

WELL, HEALTHY—The "5" hands are placed on the chest near the shoulders and brought forward into "S" positions. (11)

> IDEA: *The body is strong.*

BUSY—Place the wrist of the right "B" hand (palm facing forward) on the side of the left wrist and move the right hand back and forth slightly. (For correct position see "BUSINESS.")

LAZY—Strike the right "L" against the left shoulder. (12)

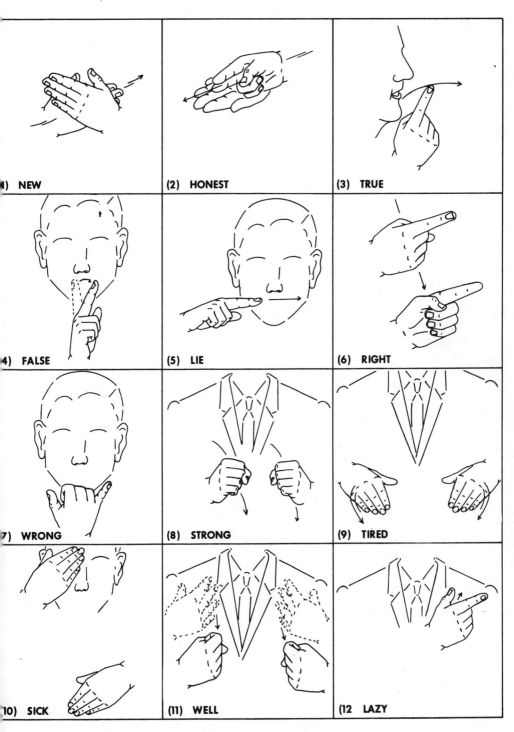

(1) NEW

(2) HONEST

(3) TRUE

(4) FALSE

(5) LIE

(6) RIGHT

(7) WRONG

(8) STRONG

(9) TIRED

(10) SICK

(11) WELL

(12 LAZY

Note: Refer to description for explanation and synonyms.

PRETTY, BEAUTIFUL—Place the right "AND" hand before the chin, palm facing you; open the fingers and circle the hand before the face from right to left ending in the original position. (1)

> IDEA: Attention is drawn to the face.

UGLY—Cross index fingers before the nose, palm facing palm; then pull them apart and bend the index fingers as they cross the face. (2)

> IDEA: Face is pulled out of shape.

THIN, LEAN—Touch right cheek with the right thumb and left cheek with right index finger; draw the hand in this position down the cheek. (3)

> IDEA: Indicates hollow cheeks.

FAT—The curved "5" hands face the cheeks and are then drawn slightly away from the face to indicate puffy cheeks. (4)

CLEAN, NICE—The right open palm is placed on the left open palm and is passed across it. (5)

> IDEA: All the dirt is rubbed off.

DIRTY—The back of the right hand is placed under the chin and the fingers wiggle. (6)

HOT—Place the right "C" at the mouth, palm facing in; give the wrist a quick twist so that the palm faces out. (7)

> IDEA: Something hot quickly taken from the mouth.

WARM—Place the "A" hand before the mouth, palm in, and open the hand gradually as it moves slightly up and out. (8)

COLD—Shake both "S" hands, palms facing each other.

> IDEA: As if shivering.

PLEASANT, COOL—Place open hands before you at shoulder height, palms toward self; bend and unbend the hands several times. (9)

DIFFERENT, VARIOUS—Cross the index fingers and pull them apart, palms facing forward. (10)

SAME—Place both index fingers side by side, palms down. (11)

OPPOSITE—Both index fingers, pointing toward each other, are pulled apart. (12)

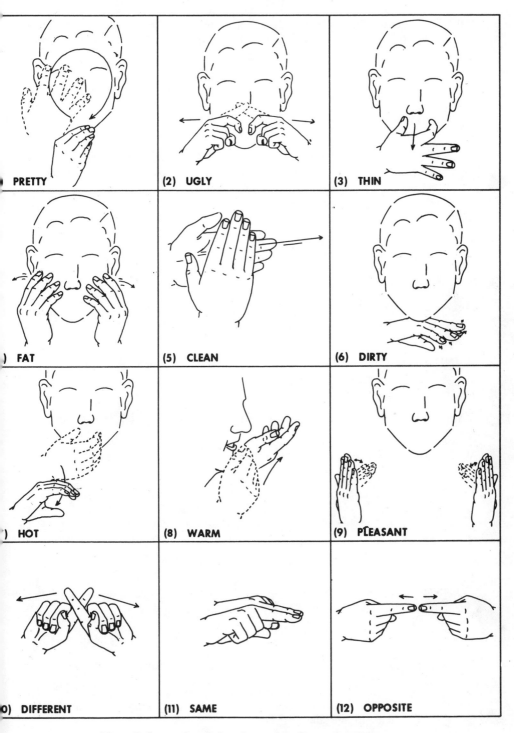

PRETTY

(2) UGLY

(3) THIN

) FAT

(5) CLEAN

(6) DIRTY

) HOT

(8) WARM

(9) PLEASANT

0) DIFFERENT

(11) SAME

(12) OPPOSITE

Note: Refer to description for explanation and synonyms.

IDLE, HOLIDAY, VACATION—Place the thumbs of the "5" hands at the armpits and wiggle the four fingers. (1)

> IDEA: A man is standing with thumbs under his suspenders.

DARK—The open hands, palms facing self and pointing up, are crossed before the face. (2)

> IDEA: Indicates darkness when eyes are covered.

LIGHT, CLEAR, PLAIN, BRIGHT—Both "AND" hands point forward, index tips touching; open the fingers as the hands are moved upward and to the sides ending in a "5" position, palms facing forward. (3)

> IDEA: Opening of the fingers indicates rays of light.

SHINING—Open palms facing each other with tips pointing up are drawn apart to the sides while the fingers are wiggling. (4)

> IDEA: Movement of the fingers represents light shining.

OBSCURE, BLURRY—Rub the right palm back and forth against the left palm, both hands in the "5" position, the back of the right hand facing self.

BLIND—Place the bent "V" before the eyes, palm in, and draw down slightly. (5)

> IDEA: Eyes pulled shut.

TAME, PET—Stroke the back of the left hand with the palm of the right hand.

WONDERFUL—Throw both open hands up, palms facing forward. (6)

INTERESTING—Make the sign for "LIKE" with both hands, one above the other, (i.e., place the thumb and index finger against the chest, with other fingers extended, and draw the hand away from the body, closing the index and thumb). (7)

> IDEA: The heart is drawn toward the object.

BORING, TEDIOUS—Place the tip of the index finger against the side of the nose and twist it slightly.

> IDEA: Nose to the grindstone.

PROMINENT, CHIEF, HIGH—Lift the right "A" hand, thumb pointing up.

FAMOUS—Index fingers touch the lips and move away from the face describing small circles in the air. (8)

> IDEA: It has been told abroad.

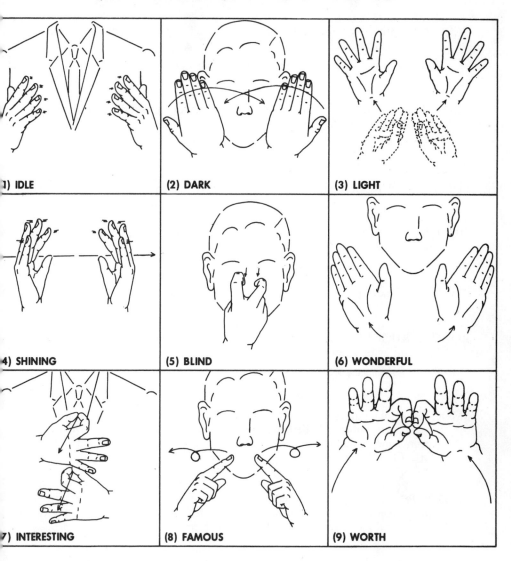

(1) IDLE   (2) DARK   (3) LIGHT

(4) SHINING   (5) BLIND   (6) WONDERFUL

(7) INTERESTING   (8) FAMOUS   (9) WORTH

Note: Refer to description for explanation and synonyms.

WORTH, WORTHY, PRECIOUS, VALUABLE, IMPORTANT, MERIT—Draw
the "F" hands up from the sides toward the center until they touch. (9)

WORTHLESS—Sign "WORTH" and drop open hands from center to sides.

PERFECT—Bring the middle fingertips of the "P" hands toward each other until they touch. (1)

> IDEA: As if "hitting the nail on the head" with the initial letter.

FINE—Place the thumb of the "5" hand at the chest, palm facing left, and move the hand slightly up and forward. (2)

> IDEA: Representing the ruffles formerly worn by gentlemen and ladies.

POLITE, COURTEOUS, FANCY—Repeat the sign for "FINE" several times.

HUNGRY—Place the "C" hand just below the throat, palm facing in, and draw it down. (3)

THIRSTY—Draw the tip of the index finger down the throat. (4)

ROUGH, RUGGED—Place the right palm against the left palm and move it forward with a wavy motion.

> IDEA: Indicating the surface is rough.

SMOOTH—Hold out both "AND" hands and draw the thumb along the tips of the fingers, moving both hands slightly away from each other. Or, place the open hands palm to palm at right angles and draw the right one across the left. (The latter usually refers to surface.) (5)

SHARP—Pass the tip of the middle finger of the right hand along the little-finger edge of the left open hand as if feeling a sharp edge and give the right hand a quick turn so that the palm faces down.

DULL (edge)—Strike the little-finger edge of the left open hand with the index-finger edge of the right "B" hand. (6)

> IDEA: The edge of the hand is dull.

DEEP—Using the right index position, push the side of the index finger straight down along the inside of the left palm which is facing right with fingertips pointing forward. (7)

> IDEA: The finger moving down indicates the depth.

SHALLOW—Sign "DEEP" and then push the open hands toward each other and back several times. Or, sign "DEEP" and "LITTLE."

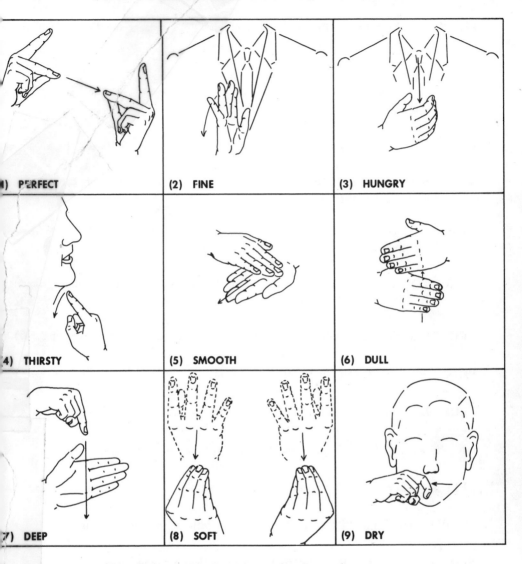

(1) PERFECT	(2) FINE	(3) HUNGRY
(4) THIRSTY	(5) SMOOTH	(6) DULL
(7) DEEP	(8) SOFT	(9) DRY

Note: Refer to description for explanation and synonyms.

SOFT—Both open "AND" hands pointing upward draw down into the "AND" position. (8)

> IDEA: As if feeling something soft between the fingers and thumb.

WET—Sign "WATER" ("W" at right side of mouth) and "SOFT."

DRY—Bent right index finger is drawn across the lips from left to right. (9)

> IDEA: The lips are dry.

FUNNY, HUMOROUS—Brush the tips of the "N" fingers off the end of the nose. (1)

AWFUL, FEARFUL—Hold the "O" hands at the sides of the face and direct them upward while opening the hands into "5" positions, the palms facing in. (2)

SWEET—Draw the fingertips down across the mouth. (See "SUGAR.")

SOUR, BITTER—Place the right index fingertip in the corner of the mouth, giving appropriate expression. (3)

QUIET, CALM—Place the index finger against the mouth, palm facing left; draw both open hands down and toward the sides, palms facing down. (4)

NOISY, SOUND, VIBRATION—Touch the tip of the ear with the index finger; direct both "5" hands toward the left, right behind left, palms down. (5)

RED—Draw the inside tip of the right index finger down across the lips. (6)

PINK—Draw the middle finger of the "P" hand down across the lips.

BLUE—Draw the "B" hand to the right with a shaking motion. (7)

GREEN—Draw the "G" hand to the right with a shaking motion.

YELLOW—Draw the "Y" hand to the right with a shaking motion.

PURPLE—Draw the "P" hand to the right with a shaking motion.

BROWN—Draw the "R" hand to the right with a shaking motion. Or draw the index-finger side of the "B" hand down the right cheek.

WHITE—Place fingertips of the open "AND" hand against the chest and draw the hand forward into the "AND" position. (8)

BLACK—Draw the index finger across the right eyebrow from left to right. (9)

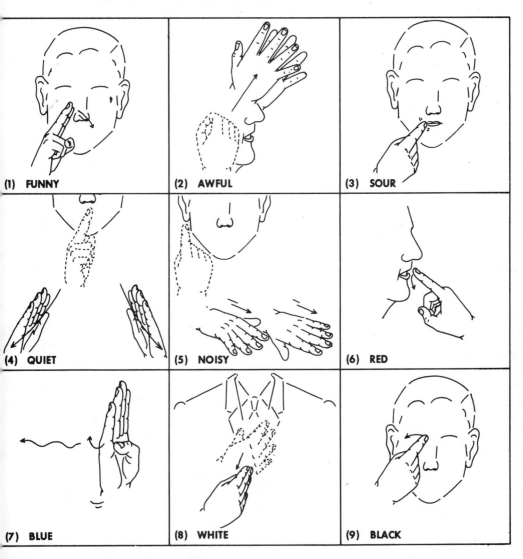

(1) FUNNY

(2) AWFUL

(3) SOUR

(4) QUIET

(5) NOISY

(6) RED

(7) BLUE

(8) WHITE

(9) BLACK

Note: Refer to description for explanation and synonyms.

CHAPTER XIII

MISCELLANEOUS NOUNS

PEOPLE—Using both "P" hands, circle them alternately toward the center. (1)

PERSON—With both hands in the "P" position bring the hands down before the body a little distance apart.

"PERSON" ENDING (Making a noun out of a verb using the ending given here) —Both open hands facing each other are brought down the sides of the body. Example: To the sign for "TEACH," add the above sign which will then make it "TEACHER." (2)

INDIVIDUAL—Both open hands facing each other are brought down before the body a short distance apart. Repeat, moving the sign slightly to the right.

NEIGHBOR—Sign "NEAR" and add the "PERSON" ending.

FRIEND—Hook the right "X" over the left "X" which is palm-up and repeat in reverse. (3)

ENEMY—Sign "OPPOSITE" (index fingers pointing toward each other are pulled apart) and add the "PERSON" ending.

SWEETHEART—Place both "A" hands together, palms facing the body; bend and unbend the thumbs. (4)

SECRETARY—Take an imaginary pencil from the ear, write into the left hand and make the "PERSON" ending.

TREASURER—Sign "MONEY" and "KEEPER."

PRESIDENT, SUPERINTENDENT—Place both "C" hands before the forehead, palms facing forward; draw them to the sides closing into "S" positions. (5)

PRINCIPAL—Circle the right "P" (counterclockwise) over the left open hand which is palm down.

GOVERNOR, GOVERNMENT—Using the right index finger, describe a small circle on the right side of the temple and end by placing the point against the temple. (6)

KING—Place the right "K" against the left shoulder, then against the right waist. (7)

QUEEN—Use the above sign with a "Q."

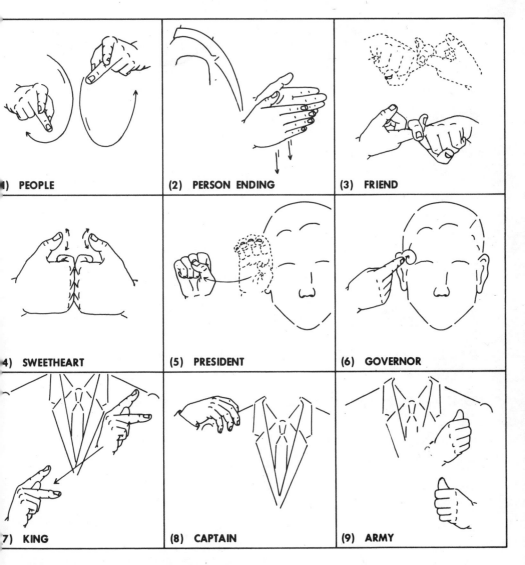

(1) PEOPLE	**(2) PERSON ENDING**	**(3) FRIEND**
(4) SWEETHEART	**(5) PRESIDENT**	**(6) GOVERNOR**
(7) KING	**(8) CAPTAIN**	**(9) ARMY**

Note: Refer to description for explanation and synonyms.

PRINCE—Use the above sign with a "P."

CAPTAIN, OFFICER—Place the curved "5" hands on shoulders. (8)

> IDEA: Epaulets on the shoulders of a uniform.

ARMY, SOLDIER—Place the right "A" against the left shoulder, palm facing body, and the left "A" on the left side of the waist. (9)

> IDEA: Soldier presenting arms.

WAR, BATTLE—Place the bent "4" hands before the body, fingertips pointing toward each other, back of the fingers up; move the hands first to the right, then to the left before you. (1)

POLICE—Place the right "C" at the left shoulder, palm facing left.

DOCTOR—Place the right "M" on the inside of the left wrist.

NURSE—Place the right "N" on the left wrist.

THIEF, ROBBER—Use both "N" hands and stroke across the upper lip to the sides. (2)

FARMER—Sign "FARM" and add the "PERSON" ending.

HYPOCRITE, IMPOSTOR, HUMBUG—Place the right open hand on the back of the left open hand; bend both hands together. (3)

NAME—Place the middle finger of the right "H" across the index finger of the left "H." (4)

NAMED, CALLED—Sign "NAME" and move the hands in this position slightly up-forward-down.

HOME—Place the tips of the "AND" hand against the mouth and then on the cheek. (5)
> IDEA: Eating and sleeping.

GROUP, CLASS—Place the "C" hands before you, draw them apart, to the sides and around to the front until the little fingers touch. (6)

HOUSE—Place the tips of the open hands together and then trace the form of a roof. (7)

CITY—Touch the tips of the open hands together as for "HOUSE" and repeat several times moving to the right.
> IDEA: A row of houses.

TENT—Place the tips of the "V" hands together and draw them down and apart to indicate the shape of a tent. (8)

CAMP—Place the tips of the "V" hands together as in "TENT" and repeat several times while moving the hands to the right.

BED—Place the right open hand on the right cheek and bend the head slightly to the right.
> IDEA: Head on a pillow.

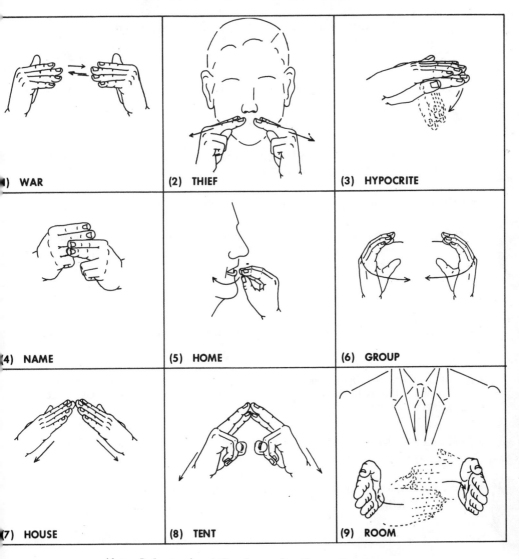

(1) WAR	(2) THIEF	(3) HYPOCRITE
(4) NAME	(5) HOME	(6) GROUP
(7) HOUSE	(8) TENT	(9) ROOM

Note: Refer to description for explanation and synonyms.

CHAIR—Sign "SIT."

ROOM—Place the open hands before you, palms toward self, left hand closest to the body; then place open hands a distance apart, palms facing each other. (This sign is often made with "R" hands instead of open hands.) (9)

IDEA: Indicates the four sides of a room.

DOOR—Place the index finger edges of the "B" hands together, palms facing forward; swing the index side of the right hand back and forth. (1)

TABLE—Point down with both index fingers, move hands toward self and point down again; place open hands side by side, palms down, draw them to the sides.

> IDEA: Indicates the four legs and top of the table.

GATE—Point the tips of the "5" hands toward each other, palms facing self, and swing the right "5" hand in and out.

MIRROR—Hold the right open hand before the face and shake it slightly.

PICTURE, PHOTOGRAPH—Place the right "C" at the side of the chin, palm facing forward; then place the "C," palm still facing forward, against the left open palm. (2)

FLAG—Place the right elbow into the left palm and wave the right hand. (3)

KEY—Place the knuckle of the crooked right index finger into the left palm and turn. (4)

CANDLE—Place the tip of the left index finger which is pointing up against the heel of the right open hand which is in an open position, palm left and fingers wiggling. (5)

UMBRELLA—Place right "S" above left "S" as if both hands are holding an umbrella; raise the right "S."

SOAP—Draw the end of the right open hand downward several times in the palm of the left.

SPOON—Place the tips of the right "H" against the left palm and lift; repeat several times.

FORK—Place the tips of the right "V" against the left palm.

KNIFE—Place the middle finger of the right "H" on the left inaex and slide it off the edge several times.

NAPKIN—Using the fingertips as a napkin, wipe the lips.

CUP—Place the little-finger edge of the right "C" on the left palm. (6)

GLASS—Sign "CUP" and raise the "C" to indicate a tall glass.

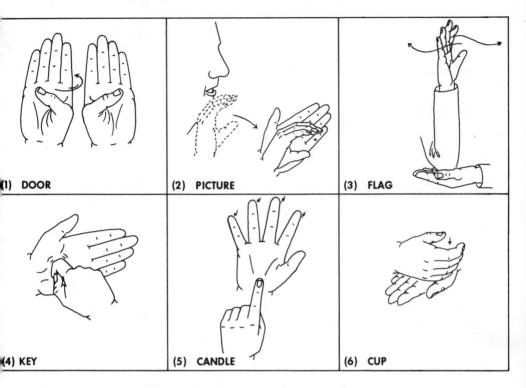

(1) DOOR

(2) PICTURE

(3) FLAG

(4) KEY

(5) CANDLE

(6) CUP

Note: Refer to description for explanation and synonyms.

TOOTHBRUSH—Using the index finger as a brush, imitate the motion of brushing the teeth.

PORCELAIN—Strike the front teeth with the fingernail of the right curved index finger.

BASKET—Place the right index finger under the wrist of the left arm, describe a semicircle and place it near the elbow.

ROPE—Place the fingertips of the "R" hands together and draw them apart with a slight wavy motion.

STRING, THREAD—Place the tips of the "I" fingers together and draw them apart with a slight wavy motion.

BUTTON—Place the "O" hand (with the other three fingers open) against the chest, palm facing left; repeat several times, lower each time.

BODY—Place the flat hands on the chest then again slightly lower. (1)

EAR—Point to the ear.

EYE—Point to the eye.

NOSE—Point to the nose.

MOUTH—Point to the mouth.

FEET—Point down twice.

ARM—Pass the back of the fingertips down the left arm.

HEAD—Place the fingertips of the bent hand at the side of the head near the temple and then slightly lower. (2)

FACE—Using the index finger, trace a circle before the face. (3)

HANDS—Stroke the back of the left hand with the right and reverse.

BEARD (Long)—Place the open "AND" hand under the chin and draw it down to a closed position, back of the hand down.

BEARD (in need of shave)—Stroke the face with the thumb on the right cheek and the fingers on the left cheek.

LIFE—Place the "5" hands, palms facing the body near the waist and draw the hands up, wiggling the fingers slightly. (4)

OPERATION—Make a short stroke along the side of the body with the tip of the right "A." (5)

HEART—Trace the form of the heart on the body with index fingers. (6)

CHARACTER—Describe a circle over the heart with the right "C" hand, palm facing left. (7)

PERSONALITY—Describe a circle over the heart with the right "P" hand, palm facing left.

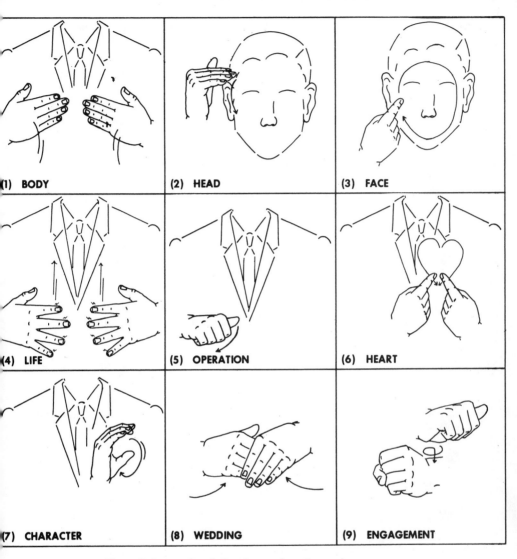

(1) BODY (2) HEAD (3) FACE

(4) LIFE (5) OPERATION (6) HEART

(7) CHARACTER (8) WEDDING (9) ENGAGEMENT

Note: Refer to description for explanation and synonyms.

WEDDING—With palms facing the body and fingers pointing down, bring the right hand into the left between the thumb and index finger. (8)

ENGAGEMENT (to be married)—Place the right "E" on the fourth finger of the left hand.

ENGAGEMENT, APPOINTMENT—Make a small circle with the right "A" hand and then place the wrist on the wrist of the left "S" which is facing right. (9)

MONEY—Strike the left palm with the back of the right "AND" hand several times. (1)

BUSINESS—Place the right "B" hand, pointing up, at the left wrist and strike several times. (2)

PROFIT—Place the thumb and index tips of the right "F" into an imaginary breast pocket. (3)

DOLLARS, BILLS—Place the right thumb inside and the fingers outside of the left open hand; draw the right hand out several times.

> IDEA: Counting bills.

COINS—Draw a small circle in the left palm with the right index.

CENTS (Used with a number)—Touch the forehead and follow by making the desired number.

COST, PRICE, CHARGE, FINE, TAX—Place the left palm before you facing right; strike the right crooked index finger against the left palm and down, palm facing self. (4)

SCHOOL—Clap the hands twice indicating a teacher's clapping for attention in the classroom.

COLLEGE—Clap the hands once, then circle the right open hand, palm down, counterclockwise above the left palm. (5)

GALLAUDET (COLLEGE FOR THE DEAF IN WASHINGTON, D. C.)—Place the right "G" hand at the side of the eye and draw back, closing the fingers. (6)

GLASSES—Draw the index finger and thumb together and back to indicate the frame of the glasses. See illustration for "Gallaudet" above.

BOOK—Place the open hands palm to palm, then open them as if opening a book. (7)

EXAMINATION, TEST—Draw question marks in the air with both index fingers, then direct the fingers of both "5" hands forward. (8)

LESSON—Hold the left palm before you; strike the little-finger edge of the right open hand across the fingers of the left and then again across the lower palm. (9)

LIST—Use same position as in "LESSON" but strike the right hand against the left several more times, moving farther down each time.

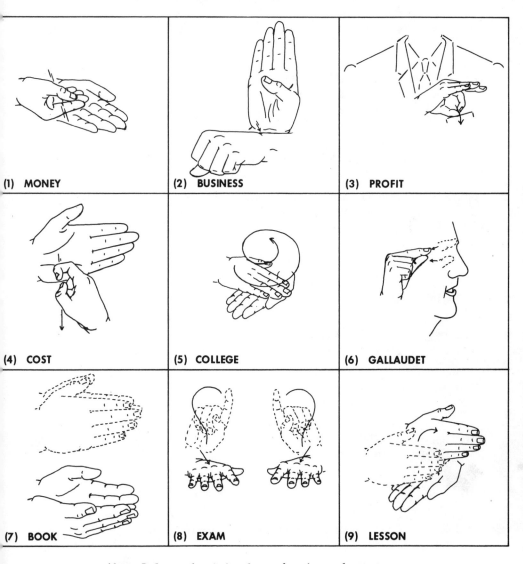

(1) MONEY

(2) BUSINESS

(3) PROFIT

(4) COST

(5) COLLEGE

(6) GALLAUDET

(7) BOOK

(8) EXAM

(9) LESSON

Note: Refer to description for explanation and synonyms.

LAW—Place the right "L" with palm facing forward, against the palm of the left hand. For "LAWYER" add the "PERSON" ending.

RULES, REGULATIONS—Place the side of the right "R" against the left open palm which is pointing up; move the right "R" down and strike again.

PERIOD, COMMA, SEMICOLON, ETC.—Use the modified "A" position as in "WRITE," and draw the desired punctuation mark in the air.

FOUNDATION—Place the right "S" under the left "S," then under the left forearm. (1)

REFUGE, SHELTER, SHIELD—Place the "S" hands before you, left behind right and push them slightly away; change the right to an open hand position with the palm facing out and move it clockwise as if shielding the left fist. (2)

INSTITUTION—Make a small clockwise circle with the right "I" and place it on the back of the left closed hand.

BUILDING—Place one hand on the other, then reverse and repeat several times, raising the sign a little each time; finish the sign by outlining the top and sides of a building. For the verb form, use the first part of this sign only.

HOSPITAL—Make a small cross on the left upper arm with the right "N." (3)

MEDICINE—Rub the tip of the right middle finger in the left palm.

JAIL—Place the back of the right "4" hand crosswise against the palm of the left "4" to indicate the bars on a jail window. (4)

FUNERAL, PROCESSION—Place the right "V" behind the left "V," both palms facing forward and move them forward, tips pointing up.

BRIDGE—Place the tips of the right "V" under the left wrist and again against the arm farther to the left.

CAR, DRIVE—Hold an imaginary steering wheel as if driving.

COLLISION—Bring the knuckles of the "S" hands forcibly together (palm-side toward the body).

TRAIN—Rub the right "H" back and forth on the back of the left "H" both palms down. (5)

WAGON, CARRIAGE, CHARIOT—Point both index fingers toward each other and circle them forward; hold imaginary reins with both modified "A" hands.

SHIP—Place the right "3" hand into the left palm and move the hands to indicate the motion of waves. (6)

BOAT—Place the little-finger edge of the open hands together to form a boat and move the hands indicating the motion of the waves. (7)

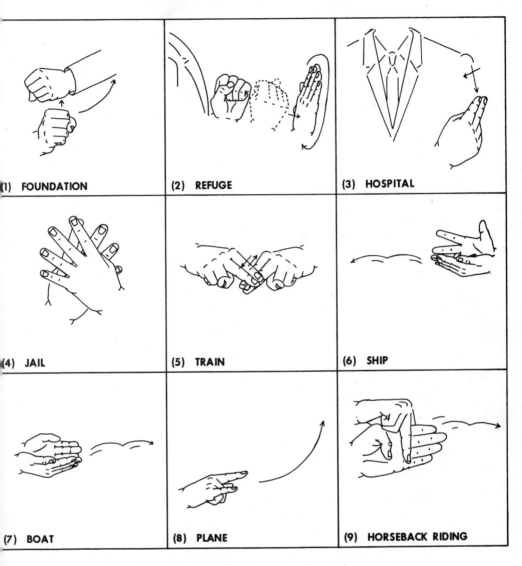

(1) FOUNDATION (2) REFUGE (3) HOSPITAL

(4) JAIL (5) TRAIN (6) SHIP

(7) BOAT (8) PLANE (9) HORSEBACK RIDING

Note: Refer to description for explanation and synonyms.

PLANE, FLY—Extend the thumb, index and little finger of the right hand and move the hand forward and up, palm facing down. (8)

HORSEBACK RIDING—Straddle the index side of the left open hand with the index and middle fingers of the right and move the hands up and down in this position. (9)

WAY, ROAD, PATH—Place both open hands before you, fingers pointing forward and palms facing each other; move both hands forward with a slight zigzag motion. (1)

PLACE—Touch the tips of the middle fingers of the "P" hands; draw them apart, circle toward self and touch the fingertips again. (This sign may also be made with the "A" hands.) (2)

ISLAND—Touch the tips of the "I" hands and complete as in "PLACE."

MOVIE—Place the palm of the right "5" hand against the palm of the left "5" and move it back and forth slightly. (3)
> IDEA: The shimmering effect of the screen.

GOLD—Touch the right ear with the index finger and bring it forward with a quick twist into a "Y" hand. (4)
> IDEA: Worn on the ear and yellow.

IRON—Bring the right "S" down and strike against the left index and off.

ELECTRICITY—Bend the index and middle fingers of both hands and strike the joints together.

RUBBER—Stroke the side of the right "X" down along the side of the chin.

WOOD—Place the little-finger side of the right open hand on the back of the left open hand and make a sawing motion. (5)

FIRE, BURN—Place the bent hands before the body, palms facing up; with the fingers wiggling move first one hand upward, then the other. (6)
> IDEA: Flames rising.

CHAIN—Link together the index and thumb of each hand (other fingers extended); repeat several times first with the index side of the right hand up, then with the thumb side up. (See illustration for "JOIN.")
> IDEA: Fingers joined as the links of a chain.

MACHINE—Lock the fingers of the curved "5" hands, palms facing self and shake them up and down. (7)
> IDEA: Gears in motion.

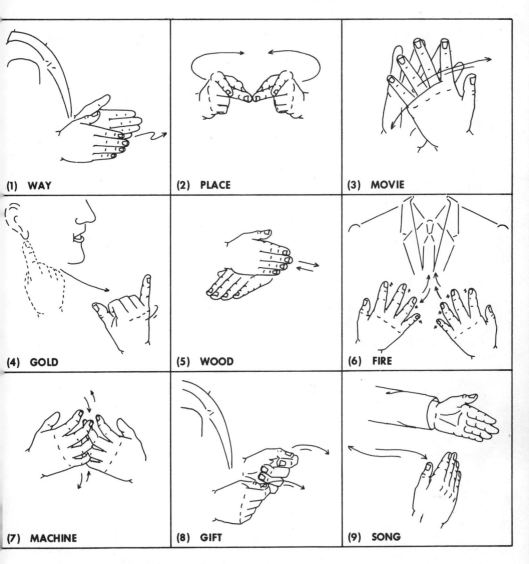

(1) WAY	(2) PLACE	(3) MOVIE
(4) GOLD	(5) WOOD	(6) FIRE
(7) MACHINE	(8) GIFT	(9) SONG

Note: Refer to description for explanation and synonyms.

GIFT, REWARD—Place both modified "A" hands before you, right behind left (right palm facing left and left palm facing right); move hands up-forward-down. (8)

SONG, SING, MUSIC—Extend the left arm; pointing the fingertips of the right hand to the left palm, wave the right arm back and forth. (9)

> IDEA: As if directing music.

POEM—Sign "SONG" using the "P" hand.

WORD—Place the right index and thumb (with other fingers closed) against the left index which is pointing up, palm facing right. (1)

SECRET—Place the thumbnail of the right "A" against the lips. (2)

BURDEN, RESPONSIBILITY—Place both hands on the right shoulder. The sign for "RESPONSIBILITY" is often made by placing the "R" hands on the shoulder. (3)

THING—Place the slightly curved open hand before you, palm facing up; move it to the right and drop it slightly. (4)

DUTY—Place the right "D" on the back of the wrist of the left closed hand. (5)

TRIUMPH, VICTORY—Use the right modified "A" as if holding a banner and swing it around above the side of the head. (This sign is often made with the right "V" hand for "VICTORY.") (6)

CONGRATULATIONS—Sign "GOOD" and then clap the hands to indicate praise.

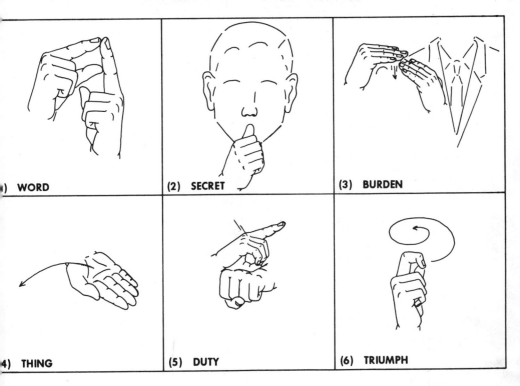

(1) WORD   (2) SECRET   (3) BURDEN

(4) THING   (5) DUTY   (6) TRIUMPH

CHAPTER XIV

RELIGION

GOD—Point the "G" forward before you, draw it up and back down ending with the open palm facing left. (1)

JESUS—Place the tip of the middle finger of the right open hand into the left palm and reverse. (2)

> IDEA: Indicating the nail prints.

CHRIST—Place the right "C" at the left shoulder and then at the right waist. (The sign for "JESUS" is often used in place of this sign.)

> IDEA: Indicating the badge worn by royalty.

LORD—Place the right "L" on the left shoulder, then on the right waist.

KINGDOM—Sign "KING" and then make a counterclockwise circle with the right open hand over the left open hand, both palms down. (3)

SALVATION, SAVE—Cross the wrists with the "S" hands, as if the wrists were bound; then bring the "S" hands out to the sides turning them so the palm side is forward. (4)

> IDEA: Bound by sin and then set free.

SAVIOUR—Sign "SAVE" and add the "PERSON" ending.

REDEEMER—Cross the "R" hands before you, draw them to the sides into an "S" position and add the "PERSON" ending.

SPIRIT, SOUL, GHOST—Place the thumb and index fingertips of the right "F" hand into the left "O" and draw the right hand upward. (5)

TRINITY—Draw the right "3" hand down through the left "C" changing into a "ONE" after it has passed through the left hand; bring the "ONE" forward and up. (6)

> IDEA: Three in one.

CROSS—Draw a cross in the air with the right "C" hand (down first, then across). (7)

CROWN—Bring both "C" hands down over the head (with other fingers extended). (8)

> IDEA: Placing a crown on the head.

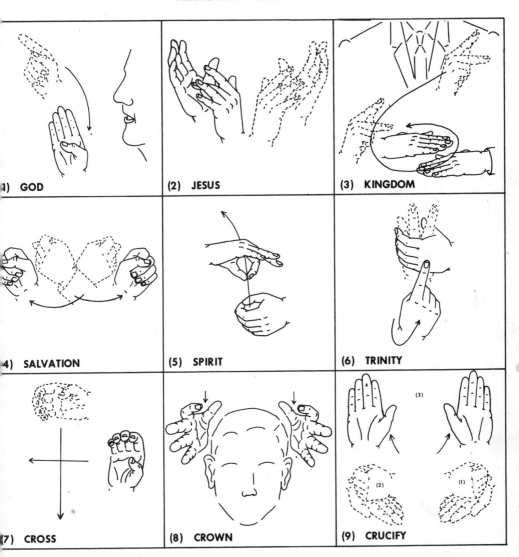

(1) GOD   (2) JESUS   (3) KINGDOM

(4) SALVATION   (5) SPIRIT   (6) TRINITY

(7) CROSS   (8) CROWN   (9) CRUCIFY

Note: Refer to description for explanation and synonyms.

RESURRECTION—Raise the right "V" from a palm-up position to a standing position on the left palm.

CRUCIFY—Place the point of the right index into the left palm and strike into the left palm with the right "S"; repeat into right hand; raise both open hands to the sides. (9)

    IDEA: *Hammering the nails into the palms with hands raised as on a cross.*

CALVARY—Sign "MOUNTAIN" and "CROSS." (Or sign only "CROSS.")

RELIGION—Place the right "R" at the heart and draw it forward, palm facing out. (1)

FAITH—Touch forehead with index finger; raise both hands slightly to the left closing them into an "S" with the right "S" resting on the left "S." (2)

FAITHFUL—Place the little-finger edge of the right "F" on the index-finger edge of the left "F"; move both hands forward and strike together again.

DISCIPLE—Sign "JESUS" and "FOLLOWER."

BACKSLIDE—Place the right "A" behind the left "A" and draw the right "A" back. (The reverse of "FOLLOW.")

PREACH—Hold the "F" hand before you and move it forward and back several times. (3)

> IDEA: "F" for "FRIARS" combined with sign for lecturing.

PRIEST—Trace a collar from the center to the side of the neck using the right thumb and index finger spread about an inch apart. (4)

PRIEST—Using the index fingers, trace the form of the breastplate worn by the priests of the Old Testament. (5)

MISSIONARY—Describe a circle over the heart with the right "M" hand, palm facing left.

PROPHESY, PROPHECY—Make the sign for "LOOK" passing it under the left open hand, palm down. (6)

PROPHET—Sign "PROPHESY" and add the "PERSON" ending.

VISION—Make the sign for "SEE" and let it pass under the left open hand, palm down.

HOLY—Make an "H," then pass the right palm across the left palm. (7)

DIVINE—Hold up the right "D" hand, then pass the right palm across the left palm.

RIGHTEOUS—Make an "R" and draw the right palm across the left palm.

PURE—Make a "P" and pass the right palm across the left palm.

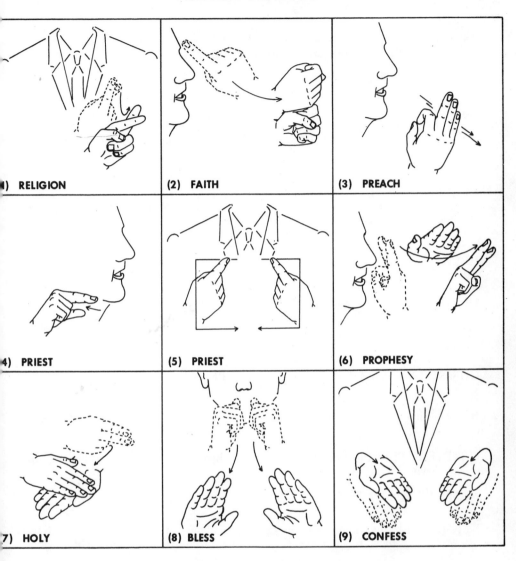

(1) RELIGION   (2) FAITH   (3) PREACH

(4) PRIEST   (5) PRIEST   (6) PROPHESY

(7) HOLY   (8) BLESS   (9) CONFESS

Note: Refer to description for explanation and synonyms.

BLESS—Place both "A" hands before the mouth, palm toward palm; bring the hands forward slightly, open them and bring them down. (8)

> IDEA: Holding the hands over an imaginary person in an act of blessing.

CONFESS, ADMIT—With fingertips pointing down, place them against the body, draw them up and forward ending with the open hands facing up before you. (9)

> IDEA: That which is within is brought out into the open.

ASCENSION—Place the tips of the right "V" hand on the left palm and raise the right "V," tips still pointing down. (1)

> IDEA: *Rising into the heavens.*

BAPTISM—1) By immersion—Using both "A" hands move them to the right in an imaginary motion of baptizing. (2)
2) By sprinkling—Hold the "S" hand over the head and then open quickly as if sprinkling water on the head.

HEAVEN—Using both open hands, palms facing in, bring them around in a circle toward self and then pass the right open hand under the left and up. (This sign is made slightly above eye level.) (3)

HELL—Point downward or spell.

DEVIL—Place the thumbs of the "3" hands on the sides of the temple; bend and unbend the index and middle fingers several times. (4)

> IDEA: *The horns of the devil.*

CHRISTIAN—Sign "JESUS" and add the "PERSON" ending.

BIBLE—Sign "JESUS" and "BOOK."

CHAPTER—Place the tips of the right "C" hand against the left palm and draw down. (5)

> IDEA: *Indicating a long passage of Scripture.*

VERSE—With the thumb and index fingers about an inch apart (other fingers closed) draw them across the left open palm from left to right. (6)

> IDEA: *A short portion as indicated by the space between the two fingers.*

GOSPEL—Sign "GOOD" and "NEWS."

CHURCH—Place the right "C" on the back of the left "S" hand. (7)

COMMUNION—Sign "WINE" and "BREAD."

SIN, EVIL—Using the index position on both hands, fingers pointing toward each other, describe simultaneous circles the right hand clockwise and the left counterclockwise. (8)

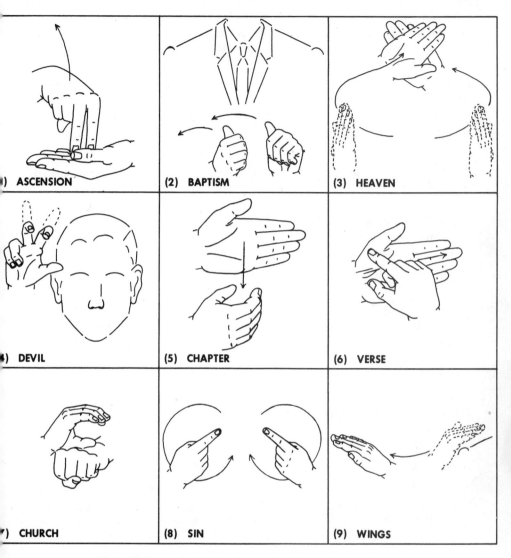

(1) ASCENSION (2) BAPTISM (3) HEAVEN

(4) DEVIL (5) CHAPTER (6) VERSE

(7) CHURCH (8) SIN (9) WINGS

Note: Refer to description for explanation and synonyms.

TRESPASS—Sign "BREAK" and "LAW."

WINGS—Place the fingertips of the right hand on the right shoulder, draw it away and then turn the hands so that the fingertips point away from the body. (9)

ANGEL—Make the above sign with two hands indicating both wings.

WORSHIP, ADORE—Place the right "A" inside the left curved hand; draw the hands up and toward self in a reverent attitude. (1)

PRAY, AMEN—Place the hands palm to palm and draw them toward the body as the head is bowed slightly.

PRAISE—Clap the hands several times.

ANOINT—Using the right "C" hand, make a motion as if pouring something over the head.

GRACE—Hold the "AND" hand over the head, bring it down and open it over the head, palm facing down. (2)

GLORY—Clap the right hand against the left, lift the right and describe a large arc before you with the right "5" hand, shaking the hand as it moves up. (3)

HALLELUJAH—Clap the hands once and make the sign for "TRIUMPH" with both hands.

MIRACLE—Sign "WONDERFUL" and "WORK."

IMAGE, STATUE, FORM—Trace an imaginary form before you with the "A" hands. (4)

IDOL—Trace an imaginary form before you with the "I" hands.

COMMANDMENTS—Hold up the left open hand, palm facing right; place the side of the right "C" against the left palm twice, the second time slightly lower than the first. (5)

CONSCIENCE, CONVICTION—Place the side of the right "G" against the heart and strike several times. (6)

    IDEA: Indicates the beating of the heart under conviction.

OFFERING—Draw the little-finger side of the right "C" across the palm toward self and sign "MONEY."

TITHE—Sign "ONE," lower the hand and sign "TEN."

ABRAHAM—Hold the left arm up with the hand near the right shoulder; strike the arm near the elbow with the right "A" hand. (7)

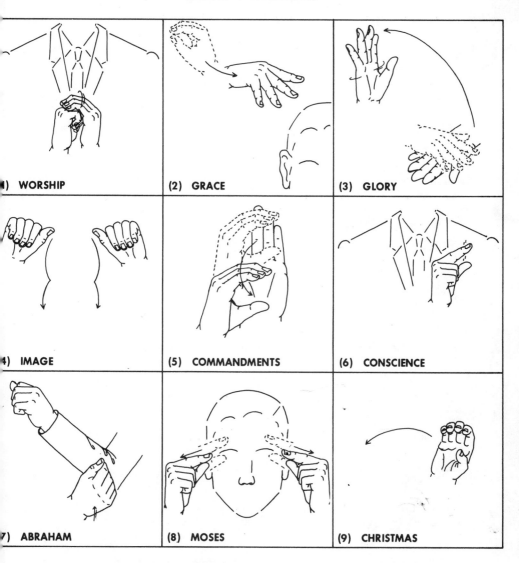

(1) WORSHIP   (2) GRACE   (3) GLORY

(4) IMAGE   (5) COMMANDMENTS   (6) CONSCIENCE

(7) ABRAHAM   (8) MOSES   (9) CHRISTMAS

Note: Refer to description for explanation and synonyms.

MOSES—Place the thumb and index finger (slightly separated) at the sides of the temple, draw them away and close them. (8)

CHRISTMAS—Describe an arc before you, using the right "C" hand. (9)

EASTER—Describe an arc before you, using the right "E" hand.

CHAPTER XV

RELIGIOUS BODIES

ASSEMBLIES OF GOD—Place the right "A" on the forehead, palm facing left; sign "GOD." (1)

BAPTIST—Sign "BAPTIZE," or: Place index-finger edge of the right open hand under the left wrist, then describe an arc and place the little-finger edge near the elbow. (2)

CATHOLIC—Using the "N" hand palm toward the face, describe a cross before the face. (3)

EPISCOPAL—Using the right index finger, describe a semicircle under the left arm from the wrist to the elbow. (4)

JEWISH—Place all the fingers on the chin, palm facing self and draw down, ending with all the fingertips touching. (5)

LUTHERAN—Place the thumbtip of the right "L" against the left palm. (6)

METHODIST—Rub the palms together, as in the sign for "ENTHUSIASM."

PRESBYTERIAN—Place the tips of the right "V" into the left palm as in the sign for "STAND."

PROTESTANT—Make the sign for "KNEEL."

QUAKER—Clasp the hands, interlacing the fingers and let the thumbs revolve about each other.

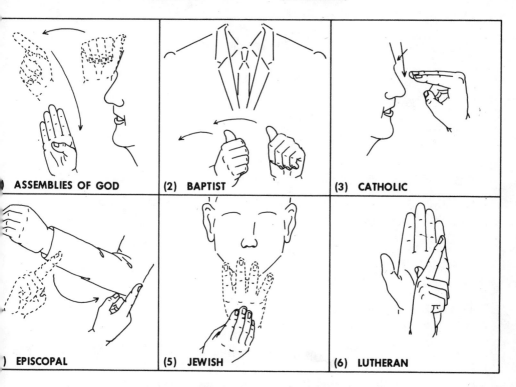

(1) ASSEMBLIES OF GOD (2) BAPTIST (3) CATHOLIC

(4) EPISCOPAL (5) JEWISH (6) LUTHERAN

Note: Refer to description for explanation and synonyms.

CHAPTER XVI

FOOD AND DRINK

FOOD—Sign "EAT" (throw the right "AND" hand lightly toward the mouth several times). (1)

MILK—Squeeze the "S" hands as if milking a cow.

CREAM—Draw the little-finger side of the right "C" hand across the left palm from the tips to the heel of the hand. (2)
>   IDEA: Skimming the cream off the milk.

COFFEE—Place the right "S" on the left "S" and make a counterclockwise grinding motion with the right "S." (3)

TEA—Place the thumb and index tips of the right "F" into the left "O" and stir with an imaginary spoon. (4)

SUGAR—Sign "SWEET" (draw the fingertips down across the mouth). (5)

BREAD—Place the left hand before the body, fingers pointing right; draw the little-finger side of the right hand down the back of the left hand several times (6)
>   IDEA: Slicing a loaf of bread.

BUTTER—Draw the tips of the right "H" hand downward across the palm of the left. (7)
>   IDEA: Buttering a slice of bread.

EGG—Strike the index finger of the left "H" with the middle finger of the right "H"; drop them and let them fall apart. (8)
>   IDEA: Breaking the shell of the egg.

MEAT—Grasp the fleshy part of the left hand (between the index and thumb) with the right index and thumb. (9)

GRAVY, OIL—Hold up the left hand, fingers pointing leftward; grasp the lower edge of the hand with the right index finger and thumb and draw down several times. (10)
>   IDEA: Gravy dripping from the meat.

SALT—Tap the back of the left "N" with the right index and middle fingers (both palms facing down). (11)

PEPPER—Use the right "O" position and imitate the motion of using the pepper shaker. (12)

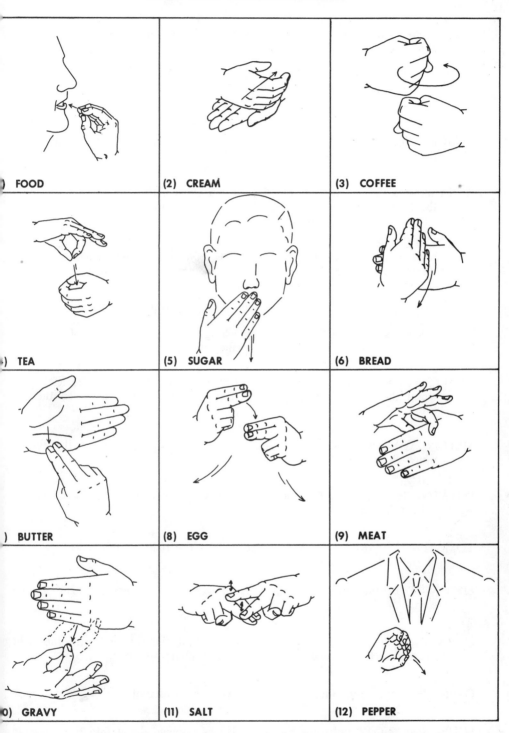

(1) FOOD   (2) CREAM   (3) COFFEE

(4) TEA   (5) SUGAR   (6) BREAD

(7) BUTTER   (8) EGG   (9) MEAT

(10) GRAVY   (11) SALT   (12) PEPPER

Note: Refer to description for explanation and synonyms.

APPLE—Press the knuckle of the index finger of the right "S" hand into the right cheek and twist. (1)

ORANGE—Draw the thumbtip of the right "Y" down the back of the left "S."

   IDEA: Cutting down the sides of the orange for peeling.

LEMON—Hold the right "S" hand before the mouth and squeeze. Or, draw the thumbtip of the right "L" down the back of the left "S."

BANANA—Go through the motion of peeling a banana, the left index representing the banana and the right fingertips pulling off the skin.

PEACH—Place the tips of the "AND" hands together as if holding a peach and break it into halves. Or, place the fingertips on the right cheek and draw them down (as in the "AND" sign), denoting the fuzz on a peach.

PEAR—Hold the left "AND" hand before you, fingertips pointing up; place the five fingers of the right hand over the left and draw the fingers up until the tips of both "AND" hands are touching; then place the tip of the right index on the left tips, representing the stem.

GRAPES—Place the slightly curved right fingertips on the back of the left hand; repeat the motion several times, each time a little farther down on the left hand.

MELON, WATERMELON, PUMPKIN—Flip the middle finger off the thumb which is resting on the back of the left "S" hand.

POTATO—Tap the back of the left "S" hand with the tips of the slightly curved right "V." (2)

TOMATO—Sign "RED," then draw the end of the right thumb down the back of the left "S" hand.

ONION—Twist the knuckle of the index finger of the right "S" hand at the corner of the eye. (3)

CORN—Hold out the left index finger to represent the cob and with the right index and thumb make the motion of shelling the corn.

CABBAGE—Strike the sides of the head with the wrists of the "A" hands.

SOUP—Sign "HOT" and using the right "H" as a spoon, dip it into the left palm and up.

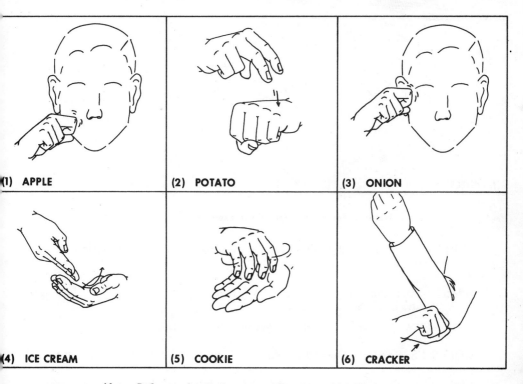

(1) APPLE	(2) POTATO	(3) ONION
(4) ICE CREAM	(5) COOKIE	(6) CRACKER

Note: Refer to description for explanation and synonyms.

ICE CREAM—Using the right "H" as a spoon, dip it into the left palm and up. (4)

COOKIE, BISCUIT—Place the tips of the right slightly curved fingers into the left palm, twist and repeat. (5)

> IDEA: Using a cookie cutter.

CAKE—Place the left open hand before you, palm facing up; slide the back of the right hand along the inside of the left palm from the tips to the heel of the hand.

DOUGHNUT—Place the tips of the right "R" at the mouth.

PIE—Place the open left hand before you palm facing up; draw the little-finger side of the right hand toward you twice as if cutting a piece of pie.

CRACKER—Strike the index finger side of the right "S" against the left arm near the elbow. (6)

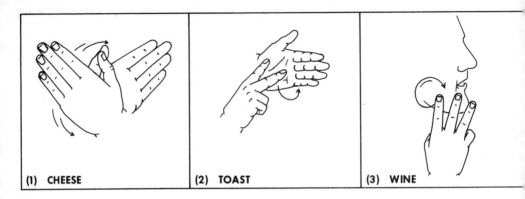

| (1) CHEESE | (2) TOAST | (3) WINE |

Note: Refer to description for explanation and synonyms.

CHEESE—Rub and twist the heel of the right open hand against the heel of the left open hand. (1)

TOAST—Place the tips of the right "V" first against the palm and then against the back of the left hand. (2)

> *IDEA: The old-fashioned method of toasting bread using a fork.*

MOLASSES, SYRUP—Draw the right index finger across the lips from left to right.

NUT—Place the thumb of the right "A" hand behind the upper teeth and draw it forward quickly.

VINEGAR—Place the index finger of the right "V" against the corner of the mouth.

WINE—Rub the right "W" in a circular motion against the cheek. (3)

LIQUOR—Place the thumb of the right "Y" hand against the mouth. For "DRUNKARD" add the "PERSON" ending.

WHISKEY—Place the right "Y" on the back of the left "S" hand.

CHAPTER XVII

CLOTHING

COAT—Trace the form of the lapels with the thumbs of the "A" hands. (1)

CLOTHING, DRESS, SUIT—Brush down the chest with the fingertips several times. (2)

SKIRT—Brush the fingertips of both hands downward and slightly outward from the waist.

TROUSERS—Draw the palms of the flat hands up against the body to the waist.

HAT—Pat the top of the head.

SHOES—Strike the sides of the "S" hands together several times. (3)

SOCKS, STOCKINGS—Place the index fingers side by side, palms down, and rub them back and forth several times. (4)

COLLAR—Using the right index and thumb slightly separated, trace the collar from the side of the neck forward to the center. (5)

NECKTIE—Using the "H" hands, tie an imaginary necktie and end with the right "H" being drawn straight down the chest.

BOW TIE—Using the "H" hands, tie an imaginary bow tie.

HANDKERCHIEF, A COLD—Place the bent index finger and thumb at the nose and draw down. (6)

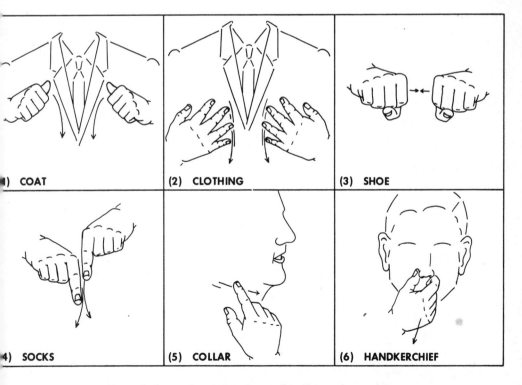

(1) COAT   (2) CLOTHING   (3) SHOE

(4) SOCKS   (5) COLLAR   (6) HANDKERCHIEF

Note: Refer to description for explanation and synonyms.

CHAPTER XVIII

ANIMALS

ANIMAL—Place the fingertips on the chest and rock the hands back and forth with the tips still resting on the chest. (1)

CAT—Place the "F" hands at the sides of the mouth and draw out to the sides representing the whiskers. (2)

DOG—Pat the leg and snap the fingers.

HORSE—Place the "H" hands at the sides of the head, palms facing forward, and move the "H" fingers up and down representing the ears of the horse. (3)

MULE—Place the open hands at the sides of the head, palms facing forward, and bend them forward and back several times representing the large ears.

COW—Place the thumbs of the "Y" hands at the sides of the head and twist the hands up. (4)

GOAT—Place the "S" hand at the chin, changing it to a "V" hand as it is placed at the forehead. (5)

SHEEP—Hold out the left arm; use the right index and middle fingers as scissors and imitate the motion of shearing on the back of the left arm. (6)

LAMB—Make the sign for "SHEEP"; then bring the open palms toward each other several times to indicate that the sheep is small.

PIG—Place the back of the right open hand under the chin and bend and unbend the hand several times. (7)

RABBIT—Place the "H" hands at the sides of the head with the palms facing back; move the "H" fingers up and down several times representing the ears of the rabbit.

TURTLE—Place the left hand on the right "A" and wiggle the right thumb to represent the head of the turtle protruding from under the shell.

FROG—Place the "S" hand at the throat and then snap out the index and middle fingers, ending in a "V" position which is pointing left.

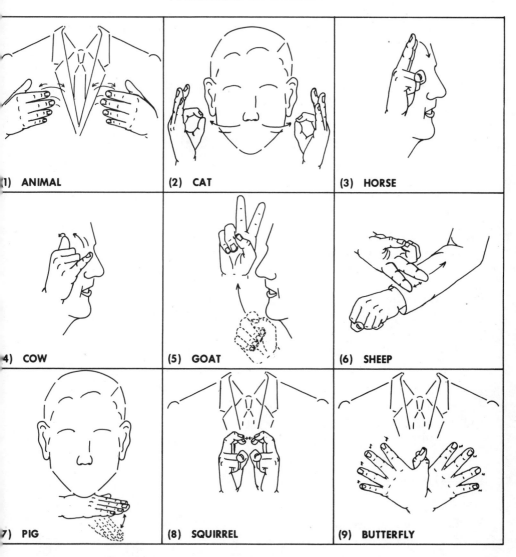

(1) ANIMAL   (2) CAT   (3) HORSE

(4) COW   (5) GOAT   (6) SHEEP

(7) PIG   (8) SQUIRREL   (9) BUTTERFLY

Note: Refer to description for explanation and synonyms.

SQUIRREL—Strike the tips of the bent "V" hands together before you several times. (8)

BUTTERFLY—Cross the "5" hands before you, palms facing the body, and lock the thumbs; wiggle the fingers. (9)

EAGLE—Hook the right "X" over the nose; flap the arms to represent wings.

BIRD—Place the index finger and thumb before the mouth representing the bill; flap the arms to represent wings. (1)

CHICKEN—Place the index finger and thumb before the mouth representing the beak; then place these fingers into the palm as if pecking at grain.

DUCK—Make a bill before the mouth (as in "CHICKEN"), using two fingers instead of one.

ROOSTER—Place the thumb of the "3" hand at the forehead. (2)

TURKEY—Place the knuckle of the right "Q" hand under the nose and shake it back and forth to represent the wattle of the turkey. (3)

OWL—Place the "O" hands before the eyes so that the eyes see through the circle of the "O"; twist them toward the center several times.

BEAR—Cross the arms placing the right hand on the left upperarm and the left hand on the right upperarm; pull the hands across the arms towards the center. (4)

ELEPHANT—Place the back of the right hand before the mouth, push up, forward and down to represent the trunk.

FOX—Place the right "F" over the nose and twist slightly. (5)

WOLF—Place the open "AND" hand before the face, fingers pointing to the face and draw them away into a closed "AND" position, representing the long nose. (6)

LION—Place the right "C" hand over the head fingers slightly separated and pointing down; move the hand back over the head in a shaking motion. This represents the lion's mane. (7)

DEER, ANTLERS—Place the thumbs of the "5" hands at the sides of the forehead and draw the hands away from the head to show the size of the horns.

CAMEL—Place the "C" hand before the neck, palm facing up; move the hand up and forward in a gentle swaying motion.

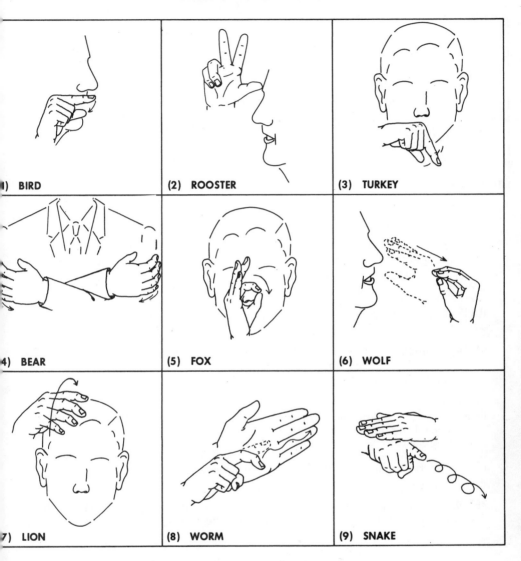

1) **BIRD** (2) **ROOSTER** (3) **TURKEY**
4) **BEAR** (5) **FOX** (6) **WOLF**
7) **LION** (8) **WORM** (9) **SNAKE**

Note: Refer to description for explanation and synonyms.

MONKEY—Scratch the sides of the body just above the waist.

WORM—Place the right index finger on the left palm and wiggle it as it moves forward to represent the worm crawling. (8)

SNAKE—Use the right "G" hand pointing forward and move it forward in a circular motion passing under the left arm. (9)

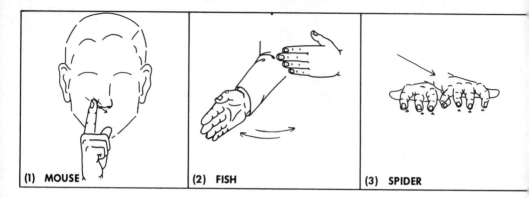

(1) MOUSE   (2) FISH   (3) SPIDER

MOUSE—Brush the tip of the nose several times with the tip of the right index finger. (1)

RAT—Brush the tip of the nose several times with the tips of the right "R."

FISH—Point the right open hand forward, palm facing left (left fingertips touching the right arm near the elbow); move the right hand back and forth to indicate the fish's tail in the water. (2)

BEE—Place the tip of the right index finger against the cheek; then brush the open hand forward as if brushing off the bee.

FLY—Use the right hand and catch an imaginary fly on the left arm.

SPIDER—Cross the curved "5" hands, palms facing down and interlock the little fingers; wiggle the fingers to represent the legs of a spider. (3)

CHAPTER XIX

SPORTS

BASEBALL—Hold an imaginary bat as if ready to hit the ball.

BASKETBALL—Hold an imaginary basketball with both hands and toss the ball.

FOOTBALL—Bring the "5" hands together, interlocking the fingers; repeat this motion several times representing the teams clashing.

VOLLEYBALL—Hit an imaginary ball over the net with both hands.

BOXING, FIGHTING—Using the "S" hands, go through the motions of boxing.

WRESTLING—Clasp the hands, locking the fingers and shake the hands back and forth from the wrists.

SWIMMING—Represent the natural motion of swimming.

ROWING—Hold imaginary oars and row.

CANOEING—With the right hand below the left as if holding a paddle, make the natural motion of paddling a canoe.

ROLLER SKATING—Hold the curved "V" fingers before you, one behind the other, palms up and move forward showing the motion of skating.

ICE SKATING—Hold the "X" hands before you one behind the other, palms up, and move forward showing the motion of skating.

BICYCLING—Use both "S" hands, palms down, and circle them forward alternately as if pedaling.

TENNIS—Hold an imaginary tennis racket and serve the ball.

PING-PONG—Hold an imaginary ping-pong paddle and move the wrist back and forth as if hitting the ball.

GOLF—Hold an imaginary golf club as if ready to strike the ball.

ARCHERY—Imitate the motion of pulling back the string of the bow.

BOWLING—Hold an imaginary bowling ball with the right hand and roll it forward.

CHAPTER XX

COUNTRIES AND NATIONALITIES

NOTE: The sign for the people of a country is made by adding the "PERSON" ending to the sign for the particular country.

NATION—Circle the right "N" over the left hand and then place it on the back of the left hand. (1)

COUNTRY—Rub the inside of the right "Y" hand in a circular motion on the left arm near the elbow. (2)

AMERICA—Interlock the fingers of both "5" hands palms facing the body and tips pointing out, and move them in a semicircle from right to left. (3)
> IDEA: The old American rail fences.

NORTH AMERICA—Describe a small circle before you with the "N" and "A."

SOUTH AMERICA—Describe a small circle before you with the "S" and "A."

UNITED STATES—Describe a small circle before you with the "U" and "S."

CANADA—Grasp the lapel with the right "A" hand.

EUROPE—Describe a small circle before you with the right "E."

ENGLAND—Place the left hand before you, palm down; grasp the outside edge of the left with the right "A," palm down. (4)

IRELAND—Circle the right "V," with the tips pointing down, over the back of the left hand and place the tips on the left. (5)

SCOTLAND—Draw the fingertips of the right "5" hand down the left upperarm; then draw the backs of the fingers across the arm away from you. (6)
> IDEA: Scotch plaid.

HOLLAND—Place the thumb of the right "Y" on the lips, then draw the hand down and out. (7)
> IDEA: The pipe used by the Dutch.

GERMANY—Cross the hands at the wrists, palms facing the body, and wiggle the fingers. (8)
> IDEA: The Double Eagle.

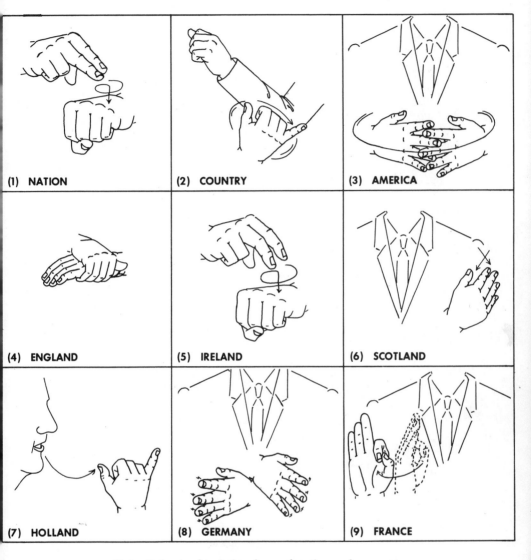

(1) NATION (2) COUNTRY (3) AMERICA

(4) ENGLAND (5) IRELAND (6) SCOTLAND

(7) HOLLAND (8) GERMANY (9) FRANCE

Note: Refer to description for explanation and synonyms.

GREECE—Draw the right "G" down the nose, palm facing left.

ROMAN, LATIN—Place the tips of the "N" fingers on the bridge and then on the tip of the nose.

FRANCE—Place the "F" before you, palm facing in; turn it so the palm faces forward moving it slightly to the right and up. (9)

SPAIN—Draw the index fingers from the shoulders to the center, hooking one over the other. (1)

ITALY—Draw a cross before the forehead with the right "I" hand, palm facing in. (2)

RUSSIA—Place the thumbs of the "5" hands on and off the waist several times. (3)

SWEDEN—Describe a circle before the forehead with the "S" hand. (4)

NORWAY—Describe a circle before the forehead with the "N" hand.

DENMARK—Describe a circle before the forehead with the "D" hand.

FINLAND—Describe a circle before the forehead with the "F" hand.

CHINA—Place the tip of the index finger at the corner of the right eye and push upward. (5)

JAPAN—Place the tip of the little finger at the corner of the right eye and push upward.

AFRICA—Use the "5" hand and place the tip of the middle finger on the nose; describe a circle before the face with the middle finger. (6)

NEGRO—Place the tips of the "N" fingers on the nose.

INDIAN—Place the tips of the thumb and forefinger of the right "F" on the nose and then on the lobe of the ear. (7)

CHAPTER XXI

CITIES AND STATES

NOTE: Many of the larger cities as well as some states have signs which are known and recognized throughout the country. However, most cities have signs which are used locally. Cities are often indicated by the use of the initial letter. Listed below are several signs for well-known cities and states.

CALIFORNIA—Touch the ear with the index finger and bring the "Y" hand forward giving it a quick twist. (See "GOLD.")

NEW YORK—Slide the right "Y" across the left palm. (8)

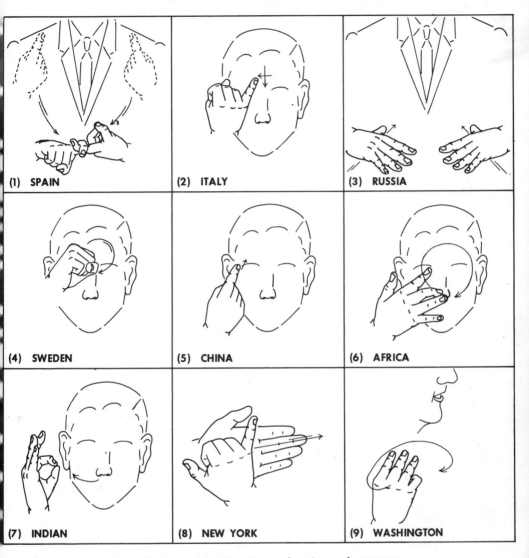

(1) SPAIN   (2) ITALY   (3) RUSSIA

(4) SWEDEN   (5) CHINA   (6) AFRICA

(7) INDIAN   (8) NEW YORK   (9) WASHINGTON

Note: Refer to description for explanation and synonyms.

CHICAGO—Draw the "C" hand down with a wavy motion.

PHILADELPHIA—Draw the "P" hand down with a wavy motion.

BALTIMORE—Move the right "B" hand forward (palm facing left and tips pointing forward).

WASHINGTON—Place the right "W" at the right shoulder, draw it up and forward. (9)

CHAPTER XXII

NUMBERS

ONE—Hold up the index finger.

TWO—Hold up the index and middle fingers.

THREE—Hold up the index finger, the middle finger, and the thumb.

FOUR—Hold up the four fingers (separated) and place the thumb against the palm.

FIVE—Hold up all five fingers.

SIX—Touch the tip of the thumb with the tip of the little finger, leaving other fingers extended.

SEVEN—Touch the tip of the thumb with the tip of the fourth finger, leaving other fingers extended.

EIGHT—Touch the tip of the thumb with the tip of the middle finger, leaving other fingers extended.

NINE—Touch the tip of the thumb with the tip of the index finger, leaving other fingers extended.

TEN—Shake the right "A" hand, thumb pointing up.

ELEVEN—Hold the "S" hand before you and snap the index finger up.

TWELVE—Hold the "S" hand before you and snap the index and middle fingers up.

Numbers from eleven to nineteen may be made by signing "TEN" and then adding the other digit. (For "TEN" the palm side faces self and for the second digit the palm faces forward.) This is illustrated on the following page for "THIRTEEN."

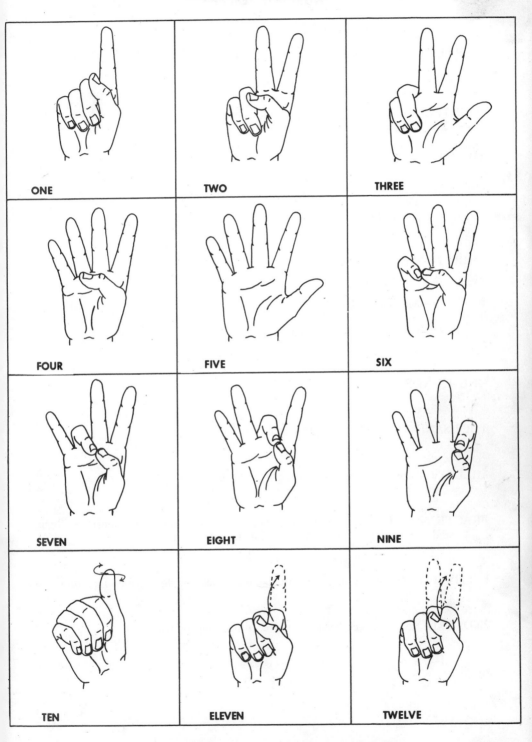

ONE

TWO

THREE

FOUR

FIVE

SIX

SEVEN

EIGHT

NINE

TEN

ELEVEN

TWELVE

Note: Refer to description for explanation and synonyms.

THIRTEEN—Sign "TEN" (palm facing in) and then "THREE" (palm facing out). (1)

FOURTEEN to NINETEEN—Proceed as above.

TWENTY—Bring the thumb and index finger together, other fingers closed. (2)

21-29—Make an "L" and add the second digit for all the twenties except 22 which is made as follows: Move the right "V" (representing "TWO") from left to right, palm facing down.

THIRTY—Make a "THREE," move it to the right and make an "O" with the three fingers. (3)

31-39—Make a "THREE," move it to the right and make the second digit.

40-99—Follow the pattern used above.

ONE HUNDRED—"ONE" and "C." (4)

THOUSAND—Place the "M" tips into the left palm. (5)

MILLION—Strike the tips of the right "M" into the left palm twice.

FRACTIONS—Make the number to indicate the numerator, lower the hand slightly and make the number to represent the denominator.

FIRST—Twist the index finger from a palm-out position to a palm-in position. (6)

2ND, 3RD, to 9TH—Proceed as above, using the proper digit.

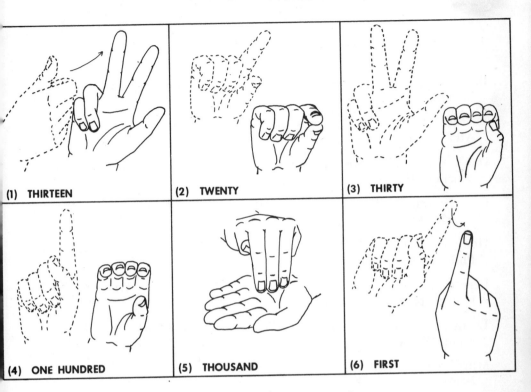

| (1) THIRTEEN | (2) TWENTY | (3) THIRTY |
| (4) ONE HUNDRED | (5) THOUSAND | (6) FIRST |

Note: Refer to description for explanation and synonyms.

PUBLICATIONS

Best, Harry, *Deafness and the Deaf in the United States.* New York: The Macmillan Co., 1943.

Boatner, Maxine Tull, *Voice of the Deaf.* Washington, D.C.: Public Affairs Press, 1959.

Davis, Hallowell, *Hearing and Deafness, A Guide for Laymen.* New York: Murray Hill Books, 1947.

Getz, Steven B., *Environment and the Deaf Child.* Springfield, Illinois: Charles C. Thomas, 1956.

Hodgson, Kenneth Walter, *The Deaf and Their Problems.* New York: Philosophical Library, 1954.

Levine, Edna S., *The Psychology of Deafness.* New York: Columbia University Press, 1960.

Levine, Edna S., *Youth in a Soundless World.* New York: New York University Press, 1956.

Murphy, Grace Emlin, *Your Deafness Is Not You.* New York: Harper, 1954.

Myklebust, Helmer R., *The Psychology of Deafness.* New York: Grune & Stratton, 1960.

Myklebust, Helmer R., *Your Deaf Child.* Springfield, Illinois: Charles Thomas, 1950.

Wright, Anna Rose, *Land of Silence,* New York: Friendship Press, Inc., 1962.

The Silent Worker, Official Monthly Publication of the National Association of the Deaf, 2495 Shattuck Avenue, Berkeley 4, Calif.

The following are available from the office of the American Annals of the Deaf, Gallaudet College, Washington 2, D. C.

American Annals of the Deaf, five issues a year. January issue contains lists of schools for the deaf, publications, teacher training centers, speech and hearing clinics, etc.

Parent Information Packet. A packet containing reprints on information pertinent for parents of deaf children.

Catalogue of publications on the education and welfare of the deaf. A catalogue containing over 150 entries.

INDEX TO SIGNS

INDEX TO SIGNS

INDEX TO SIGNS

INDEX TO SIGNS

INDEX TO SIGNS